# DAILY BIBLE STUDY GUIDE

## VOLUME I
## THE PSALMS

## BY DR. DELRON SHIRLEY

2005
REVISED 2009

COVER DESIGN BY JEREMY SHIRLEY

To obtain permission to quote material from this book, please contact:

Delron Shirley
3210 Cathedral Spires Dr.
Colorado Springs, CO 80904
teachallnations@msn.com
www.teachallnationsmission.com

# Introduction to the Series

With almost every major purchase, we receive an instruction manual to help us care for and get the most efficient use out of the product. Household appliances, automobiles, computer software programs, you name it – they all come with their owner's manuals which, by and large, are simply shelved and rarely read or consulted. Most of us just rely on the brief instructions we received on the showroom floor and what we can gain from trial-and-error usage of the product. Unfortunately, this is exactly the same way we approach our spiritual lives. We have been presented with an owner's manual to ensure that we get the best and longest-lasting results out of our spiritual lives; it's called the Bible. Unfortunately, most of us prefer to rely on a few sermons, an occasional book or tape, and a sporadic television program rather than to diligently delve into the truths of this instructional manual. Others who do try to study this manual sometimes find it confusing and simply decide not to force their way into the revelation available through the proper understanding of the book.

Maybe we aren't as bad as the pastor and church council in this little story, but it is true that we often don't get all the facts straight.

A church was interviewing the young preacher. It would be his first church. The committee asked him, "Son, do you know the Bible?" "Oh, yes," he replied, "I really know the Bible." The chairman asked, "What part of the Bible do you know best?" The young man replied, "I know the Old and New Testament – all of it!" The chairman responded, "Well, if you know so much about the Bible, why don't you tell us a story? Do you know the story of the Good Samaritan?" "Yes, sir." "Well then, you just tell us that story." "Well, there was a man of the Pharisees named Nicodemus. He went down to Jericho by night and fell upon stony ground. The thorns choked him half to death. And he said, 'What shall I do. I shall arise and go to my father's house.' And he arose and climbed up in a sycamore tree. And the next day, Sodom and his wife Gomorrah came by, and they carried him down to the ark of Moses to take care of him. As he was going through the eastern gate into the ark, he caught his hair in a limb, and he hung there for forty days and forty nights. And, afterward, he was hungered and the ravens came and fed him. And, the next day, three wise men came and carried him down to Nineveh. And when he got down there, he found Delilah sitting on a wall. And he said, 'Chunk her down boys.' And they said, 'How many times shall we chunk her down? Till seven times?' And he said, 'Nay, but until seventy times seven.' And they chunked her down 490 times. And she burst asunder in their midst and they picked up 12 baskets full of fragments. And in the resurrection, whose wife will she be?" The chairman of the committee said, "Fellows, I know he's young, but I really think we ought to call him. He really knows his Bible."

The Bible is the most extraordinary book in all of human history. It is a book which throughout history has been outlawed, confiscated, and burned by the thousands of copies. Armies have marched attempting to destroy it. Whole organizations have been created within different governments to seek out among the populace, find those people who have a Bible, and imprison them. There have been all types of legislative attempts to make this Bible disappear. In addition, some of the most astute minds of human history have written books to try to counter the Bible. Some have dedicated their entire lives to disproving this book. There has never been another book in all of human history that has been so attacked legally and philosophically. Yet, this is a book that refuses to die. It is a book that refuses to disappear. In every place where the enemy has tried to stamp it out, the Bible proliferates.

This book is definitely the most read book in all of human history. At the same time, it is the most unread book in all of human history. The reason I say this is because the Bible is continually the world's bestseller. Only once or twice has a bestseller sold more copies in a single week or month than the Bible. However, the success of these other literary works doesn't last long, and the Bible always returns as the number one bestseller shortly. It has been that way year after year after year. More people have read the Bible than any other book ever printed. But, at the same time, it is probably one of the least-read books. How many of us have Bibles sitting on the shelf collecting dust? We may have two or three Bibles for reference and another that we read daily. But how often does the copy that we claim to be reading basically sit on the shelf not being read? The Bible is likely the most unread book in all of human history because we buy copies of it, put them down, and don't read them. I heard recently that a national survey of Christians across America found that only one out of five have any kind of regular, systematic program for reading the Bible. That means that there are four times as many born-again Christians who have Bibles that basically sit around unopened. It was found that the average length of time spent reading a Bible is five minutes a day. For two out of five Christians, the only time during the week that they ever really open and read their Bibles is when they are in an organized group. They open the Bible only because the pastor or Sunday school teacher instructs them to open to a particular passage. The same study went on to say that two out of five born-again Christians don't even know for sure that the story of Jonah and the whale is part of the Bible or in which book it is found. We are dealing with a book that, even though it is the most popular book in of all of human history, is one that still remains unread and apart from our daily lives. It doesn't need to be that way.

The Bible is made up of many books. Inside, you can read history, mysteries, prophecies, poetry, and intrigue. This is a book that even has cookbook characteristics; it tells us what to eat and what not to eat. It is unique in that it takes even its greatest heroes and tells us their flaws. The Bible holds a unique record in being the most translated book in all of human history. In addition, the Bible holds the world record as the book that has been translated first into most languages. Many tribes living in the far-flung jungles and distant deserts had no written language until it was given to them by the Bible translators. These dedicated men and women study the language spoken by a tribe, transcribe it into written form, and then hand them a book to read. That book is always the Bible, the Word of God. The Bible is unique in that it has spawned literally libraries of other books. People have read this book and received insight, revelation, and inspiration. Then they have written other books on what they have found in this one book. The volumes could fill multiple libraries. Many of the most brilliant minds of human history have dedicated their lives to reading, learning, translating, and interpreting this book. This one book is a wealth of knowledge and it is a springboard for conveying all sorts of information. It not only tells us just about the battles that David won and about the anointed psalms David wrote; it also tells us about David's failures. The Bible tells us very explicitly about the lives of all its great heroes. The Bible has become the basis for human living and human government all over the world. If you look at every nation's laws, almost all of them are patterned after the Ten Commandments and Old Testament Law. It is a book that is the foundation for all of human living and all of human society.

Dr. Lester Sumrall once told the story of a man who was trying to sell Bibles in a South American community, but no one wanted to buy them. In fact, one person ripped up one of the salesman's books and threw it into the gutter to show his disdain for the book. One of the local merchants picked up the discarded Bible and used the pages to wrap up the goods he sold. When his customers unwrapped their purchases, they started to read the pages. The entire city became aflame with revival by reading the discarded pages of a torn-up book. This book is unique.

People have criticized it and called it inaccurate. But, every time it has been challenged, the Bible has emerged victorious. One of the reasons it was challenged was because it speaks of the Hittites as one of the nations the Israelites fought against when they came into the Promised Land. Because archaeologists had never uncovered any records referring to the Hittite nation, historians believed that no such people had ever lived. These scholars accused the Bible of being only a myth. In the late 1800s, archaeological proof was found which proved that the Hittites not only existed but were actually one of the greatest empires of that period of history. Before then, the only ones who knew the truth about the Hittites were those who believed the Bible. The Bible disproved the theories of the scholars and confirmed the faith of those who believed its record. The Bible tells us that King Solomon mined for iron and copper; however, in the nineteenth century geologists believed there to be no iron or copper anywhere in the land of Israel. They said that the Bible was full of contradiction and, therefore, not true. Around the turn of the twentieth century, an archeologist spent twenty years traveling throughout the Middle East looking for iron and copper because he believed the Bible. In his excavations near the Dead Sea, he uncovered a copper mine and about a dozen refineries which Solomon used to refine the copper, proving again the Bible's inerrancy. The Bible tells us that Solomon had built entire cities where his horses were housed; however, secular history bore no record of this. In the city of Megiddo, where the Battle of Armageddon will be fought, the University of Chicago excavated stalls for 450 horses. People challenged the Book of Luke because it tells us that Cyrenius was governor of Syria when Jesus was born and that Augustus was the emperor in Rome. For centuries, historians rejected this statement because Cyrenius was governor long after Augustus' death. That is – until the recent discovery of documents showing that Cyrenius was one of the few people in all of history who served in the same position two different times in his life. Historians knew about his second term as governor of Syria, but archeologists found that he also had another term years before – during Augustus' reign. Again, the Bible justified itself when men said it could not be proven. The Book of Acts, telling about Paul's going from the city of Iconium to the city of Lystra, says that Paul passed out of that country into another country. But historians, arguing that Iconium and Lystra had always been in the same country, called the Bible in error. About the end of the nineteenth century, archeologists found that at one time in history, Iconium had been annexed to a neighboring country and was not part of the same country as Lystra. That short period of time was exactly during the time that Paul traveled from Iconium and Lystra. Even though people have challenged it, the Bible has always proven itself true. History proves the Bible. Archeology proves the Bible. The Bible is without error, and man's theories have to correct themselves to align with the proven truth of the Scriptures.

> *But continue thou in the things which thou hast learned and hast been assured of, knowing of whom thou hast learned them; And that from a child thou hast known the holy scriptures, which art able to make thee wise unto salvation through faith which is in Christ Jesus.* (II Timothy 3:14-15)

Nothing else can make us wise. The Bible can make us more than wise; it can make us wise unto salvation. It illuminates our thinking and our spirits. That wisdom will lead us to one thing – salvation through God.

> *All scripture is given by inspiration of God and is profitable for doctrine, for reproof, for correction, for instruction in righteousness.* (II Timothy 3:16)

Many other books have no profit in them. But the Bible is profitable for doctrine – deciding what you believe. It is also profitable for reproof and correction. If your life is going the wrong way, it is profitable for turning you around and setting you on the right road. One great man said, "The Bible is a book that is full of contradictions. It contradicts everything that I, as an unregenerate man, want to think. It contradicts everything that I, as an unregenerate man, want to believe. It contradicts everything that I, as an unregenerate man, want to do." The Bible is a book full of contradictions. It contradicts our lives until we are born again and come into alignment with it. The Bible is profitable for instruction in righteousness. We are going to live lives full of contradiction until we begin to let the Bible instruct us in how to live. *Because I love thy commandments, it has made me wiser than mine enemies.* (Psalm 119:98) The commandments of God renew our minds and build up our inner man. They give us an edge over those who come against us because we have the wisdom of God, found only in the Bible.

> *How sweet are thy words unto my taste? Sweeter than honey to my mouth.* (Psalm 119:103)

It is amazing to me when I hear statistics that say that only one out of five Christians has any kind of disciplined regular Bible reading. I find the Bible sweet. When a box of chocolate candy is in my house, it doesn't go unnoticed. I find myself going back again and again to that candy. I am the same way with the Bible. It is sweet, and I find myself drawn back to it every day. Every day, I have to have my "charge" from that Word. I believe that every born-again person should also be the same. The Bible came from God; it is guarded and protected from error by the work of the Holy Spirit. *Howbeit when he the Spirit of Truth has come, he will guide you into all truth for he shall not speak of himself but whatsoever he shall hear, that shall he speak and he will show you things to come.* (John 16:13) The Holy Spirit inspires and leads men into truth – both those who wrote the Bible and us as we read and understand the Bible.

The Bible has been preserved in a very accurate form. For centuries before the invention of printing presses, every copy had to be written out by hand. Century after century, monks dedicated their lives to transcribing the Bible by handwriting. These scribes counted the very letters on the page; if they found that one word or one letter was missing, they would tear up the whole page – destroying a whole day's work – because there was an error. The Bible was preserved point-by-point, word-by-word for century after century. The basic texts of the Bible have been preserved for hundreds of years without any error. When the discovery of Dead Sea Scrolls gave us original copies of the Old Testament texts that pre-dated the previously known texts by almost a thousand years, almost no variances were revealed. In other words, the discovery confirmed the accuracy with which the Word of God had been preserved.

A few years ago I was sitting next to a Muslim on an airplane. When I opened my Bible and began to share my faith, the Islamic lady jumped back saying, "We never touch the Koran without first washing our hands." On another occasion, my hand baggage was being inspected by the security officer in the Ben Gurion Airport in Israel, when he discovered that I was carrying a copy of the Old Testament in Hebrew. After reprimanding me for having other books stacked on top of the Torah, he repacked my bag with the Bible in uppermost position. We must not get into this sort of bondage to the point that the Bible itself becomes an object of reverence, but we must respect the Bible for what it is – the revealed Word of God to us. It is not just a common book. It is a book that was written over 1,600 years of history by 40 different authors from all walks of life. Yet, all the books flow together to tell us the same truth.

The Bible can be proven true. Everything that it said would come to pass has come to pass. The Bible prophesied that Jesus would be born of a virgin, and He was born of a virgin. The Bible prophesied Jesus' death, and it gives some very explicit detail about the crucifixion – even down to the fact that the soldiers gambled for his clothes. These prophecies were fulfilled from the jot to the tittle. The resurrection was prophesied, and it was fulfilled. The giving of the Holy Spirit was prophesied, and that was fulfilled. Ezekiel prophesied that the city of Tyre would be destroyed. *And your very dust will be cast into the sea.* Right after Ezekiel's time, Nebuchadnezzar marched into Tyre and destroyed it exactly as Ezekiel prophesied, but he didn't throw it into the sea.

When Alexander the Great came to the ruins of Tyre almost three hundred years later, he discovered that a new city had been built just off the coast. The great conqueror swept all of the rubble left behind by Nebuchadnezzar into the sea, making a bridge for his army to march across to conquer the new city of Tyre. Even though there was a period of almost three centuries, everything happened exactly the way God said it was going to happen. Jesus prophesied that the city of Jerusalem and the Temple would be destroyed. When Titus came to assault the city of Jerusalem, he told his soldiers not to destroy the Temple. He wanted it to remain as a symbol of the great city he had conquered. Seeing the Temple covered in gold, one of Titus' infantrymen held up his flaming torch to loosen a piece of gold from the wall to slip into his pocket. The torch ignited the building and the Temple went into flames. The rest of the army then began to ravage the building, claiming their own nuggets of gold. The end result was that not one stone was left upon another. The great Roman general gave orders not to destroy the Temple, but Jesus said that it would be destroyed. The Word of God never fails. Everything that has been prophesied has been fulfilled. The Bible is the inspired Word of God. There has never been a man able to prove that the Bible is untrue. The rebirth of Israel is a biblical prophecy which we have seen in our own time. For almost two millennia, there was no nation of Israel. But – suddenly in the fullness of time – a nation was reborn. Gathered out of nations all over the world, a nation was reborn in a single day in exactly the same geographical location where God said it would happen.

The Bible is a book that speaks to lost humanity telling them about their condition, their need, and – most importantly – the answer. Speaking of the power of the Word of God, a great scholar once said: "It is time that we stop defending the lion. It is time that we let the lion out of its cage and he will defend himself." Let's not worry what the critics say. Now is the time to agree with the Bible and let it turn our lives around. If you have been one of those four out of five who do not have a daily reading schedule, then determine that today you will begin to read your Bible on a daily basis. If you are one of those who only open the Bible once a week in a church service, determine that today is the day you will begin to read the Bible every day in a systematic study. It is your owner's manual. It is reliable. It is true. It is infallible. It is necessary!

There is no question that the Christian's only guarantee for a successful spiritual life is to read and live by his owner's manual. That is exactly what this set of study manuals is designed to help you do. It is a four-year spiritual journal with a daily devotional study through the Word of God. These manuals consist of a yearlong walk through the New Testament and a three-year excursion through the Old Testament based on studying one chapter each weekday for the fifty-two weeks in a year. The expedition through the book of Psalms will be repeated annually on the weekends. Each entry includes one verse to memorize. It was difficult to select just one verse each day because many chapters contain so many verses which we should, as the psalmist said, hide in our hearts; therefore, the verse I picked should be considered a suggestion. You may wish to select another one or even opt to memorize several verses from some chapters. Next comes a short distillation of the basic principle of the chapter and a brief outline of the chapter. This study is intended to be of a rather devotional approach – although, as a teacher, I found it impossible not to expound on the scriptures occasionally and sometimes to lapse into a bona fide exegetical explanation. The Bible study is followed by a simple prayer intended to bring the truth of the chapter into practical application. A section for the reader's notes follows where you can log your own personal revelations and insights about the chapter. A space for noting your own personal spiritual journal (which could include prayer requests, answered prayers, and testimonies) rounds out the daily devotion.

I believe that twenty minutes a day, seven days a week, fifty-two weeks a year will produce one brand new man in each friend who seriously applies himself to the program and the program to himself. Welcome to your owner's manual.

This series of Bible studies is dedicated to all who have been links in the long chain which the Lord has used to transmit His Word to me: to those who wrote the words as they were inspired by the Holy Spirit – many of whom suffered misunderstanding, abuse, rejection, and imprisonment because of their revelations; to those who preserved the documents through the centuries – including the thousands who sacrificed the joys of family life and the pleasures of society to isolate themselves in monasteries tirelessly hand-copying the texts all day, every day, year after year; to those who dedicated themselves to translating the message into languages the people could read – courageous individuals who disregarded the dangers of hostile environments, relished the meticulous labor of deciphering new languages, and defied the established hierarchy which resisted and even criminalized their work; to those who have risked and even given their lives to smuggle the contraband Word of Life to the nations held in spiritual darkness by political and religious tyrants; to those who have dedicated their intelligence and insight to interpreting the truths of the Scriptures into comprehensive and understandable lessons; to those individuals and organizations who, at their own personal expense, have seen that the Book was made available to people in all walks of life; to those who have given themselves – as ministers or laymen – to proclaiming its truths; to those who introduced me to the treasures of this Book – my parents, my grandparents, my preachers, and my teachers.

Week: One

Day: Saturday

Book: Psalms

Chapter: One

Memory Verse: One

Principle: This psalm is a perfect follow-up to the book of Job in that it teaches us that God knows how to bless the righteous and bring judgment to the ungodly.

Outline:

       Verses 1-3 – Blessing and preservation are promised to the godly.

       Verses 4-5 – Judgment and destruction are the destiny of the ungodly.

       Verse 6 – The Lord knows how to distinguish and deal with both the righteous and the unrighteous.

Prayer Focus: Lord, help me to be careful to order my life according to Your ways so that I can be planted like a tree beside rivers of living water.   Amen.

Notes:

Spiritual Journal:

Week: One
Day: Sunday morning
Book: Psalms
Chapter: Two
Memory Verse: Eight
Principle: This psalm is a call for the nations of the earth to submit to the authority of the Lord. Historically, it refers to the nations which became subservient to Israel. Prophetically, it refers to the messianic kingdom and the reception of the gospel of Jesus Christ.
Outline:
Verses 1-3 – The question is raised as to why the gentiles feel that they need not submit to God's authority.
Verses 4-7 – The Lord will mock those who resist Him and affirm that He has indeed established His son as king in the earth.
Verses 8-9 – The inheritance promised to the son king is that he will receive the nations and will subdue them. This passage also symbolically promises the Body of Christ evangelical success over the nations of the world.
Verses 10-12 – The nations are advised to accept the authority of the king and receive his blessings.
Prayer Focus: Lord, more than anything else, I want to see the nations of the earth received into Your kingdom. Help me to teach them to submit to Your gospel. Amen.
Notes:

Spiritual Journal:

Week: One

Day: Sunday evening

Book: Psalms

Chapter: Three

Memory Verse: Three

Principle: No matter how many enemies rise against the believer, God's mercy will sustain and preserve him.

Outline:

Verses 1-2 – David describes the multitude which has attacked him.   Historically, this psalm refers to the uprising led by Absalom.

Verses 3-6 – David rejoiced in the preservation and deliverance from the Lord.

Verses 7-8 – A prayer of salvation is coupled with a testimony that God is, indeed, the Savior.

Prayer Focus: Lord, help me to never fear in the face of any enemy by remembering that You are my Savior.   Amen.

Notes:

Spiritual Journal:

Week: Two
Day: Saturday
Book: Psalms
Chapter: Four
Memory Verse: Eight
Principle: The question of how some can rebel against the authority of God is contrasted with the testimony of His provision for those who trust Him.
Outline:

> Verse 1 – A prayer for God to hear is coupled with the confidence of the testimony that He has provided during time of distress.
>
> Verse 2 – The question of how long men can insist upon his rebelliousness is raised.
>
> Verse 3 – The promise for God's watch care for the godly is reiterated.
>
> Verses 4-5 – The proper response to God's care is outlined.
>
> Verses 6-8 – The question concerning what goodness God shows to His followers is raised and then answered in that He gives gladness and security to the godly.

Prayer Focus: Lord, help me to always have a victorious testimony to share as an answer when the question of submission to You is raised.   Amen.
Notes:

Spiritual Journal:

Week: Two

Day: Sunday morning

Book: Psalms

Chapter: Five

Memory Verse: Four

Principle: A commitment to constant and consistent prayer is coupled with the promise of provision for those who pray and a reminder of judgment against the unrighteous.

Outline:

> Verses 1-3 – Determination to pray daily is expressed.
>
> Verses 4-6 – God's disdain for unrighteousness is described.
>
> Verses 7-8 – The psalmist determined to worship God and anticipated His directions as a result.
>
> Verses 9-10 – The corruption of the wicked and their pending judgment is delineated.
>
> Verses 11-12 – Rejoicing is in order for those who trust God.

Prayer Focus: Lord, Your love is my reason for joy and rejoicing. Never let me fail to worship and pray to You and, thus, lose my source of joy. Amen.

Notes:

Spiritual Journal:

Week: Two
Day: Sunday evening
Book: Psalms
Chapter: Six
Memory Verse: Nine
Principle: Intense prayer results in God's favorable answer.
Outline:
Verses 1-5 – The psalmist cries out for mercy.
Verses 6-7 – The intensity of intercession is described.
Verses 8-10 – The enemies are rebuked on the basis of God's having heard and answered prayer.
Prayer Focus: Lord, I know that I often fail to have the answers I need because I fail to pray or fail to pray with true intensity and sincerity. Help me to truly trust You with all my requests. Amen.
Notes:

Spiritual Journal:

Week: Three
Day: Saturday
Book: Psalms
Chapter: Seven
Memory Verse: Seventeen
Principle: Because of His own righteous nature, God will arise to judge the wicked.
Outline:

      Verses 1-2 – The psalmist expresses his trust in the Lord as a deliverer.

      Verses 3-5 – He offers himself for judgment if he has done unrighteously.

      Verses 6-8 – He asks God to avenge him based on his righteousness and integrity.

      Verses 9-13 – Because of His nature, God will bring destruction upon the wicked.

      Verses14-16 – The wicked's evil plans "backfire" on themselves and they are caught in their own traps.

      Verse 17 – God is to be praised because of His righteous judgments.

Prayer Focus: Lord, help me to always keep in mind Your righteousness as the focal point of all judgment against the wicked and deliverance on behalf of the godly. Amen.

Notes:

Spiritual Journal:

Week: Three
Day: Sunday morning
Book: Psalms
Chapter: Eight
Memory Verse: One
Principle: The excellence of God is shown in the creation and the way He has allowed man to rule it.
Outline:

> Verse 1 – God's name is excellent in heaven and earth.
>
> Verse 2 – He subdues the enemies and gives the weak reason to rejoice.
>
> Verses 3-8 – It is amazing that man has been elevated to the position of determination in the vastness of creation.
>
> Verse 9 – God's excellence is reiterated.

Prayer Focus: Lord, I do stand amazed that You pay attention to seemingly insignificant men in the vastness of Your great creation. Thank you for caring for me. Amen.
Notes:

Spiritual Journal:

Week: Three
Day: Sunday evening
Book: Psalms
Chapter: Nine
Memory Verse: Ten
Principle: It is an oft-repeated theme in Psalms and certainly worthy of repetition: God is worthy of praise because of His judgment on wickedness and deliverance for the righteous.
Outline:
 Verses 1-2 – The psalmist determines to praise God.
 Verses 3-5 – The destruction of the wicked is proclaimed.
 Verses 6-8 – God remains even after the enemies are destroyed.
 Verses 9-10 – The Lord is a refuge for those who trust Him.
 Verses 11-12 – Praise is due to God for His deliverance.
 Verses 13-16 – The psalmist will praise God and proclaim His testimony because of His mercy and deliverance.
 Verses 17-18 – The fate of the wicked and the destiny of the needy are contrasted.
 Verses 19-20 – The psalm ends with a prayer for God to act in judgment, not for judgment's sake but for the establishment of the fact that men are not God.
Prayer Focus: Lord, I exalt You in Your righteousness and trust You in Your judgments. Amen.
Notes:

Spiritual Journal:

Week: Four
Day: Saturday
Book: Psalms
Chapter: Ten
Memory Verse: Verses seventeen and eighteen
Principle: After repeatedly reaffirming the fact that God has and will judge the wicked, the psalmist cries out as to why many wicked continue to go seemingly unjudged.
Outline:
       Verse 1 – The psalmist questions why the Lord has not judged the wicked.
       Verses 2-13 – The evil deeds and injustices of the wicked are listed in context of his feeling that God is overlooking his sin.
       Verses 14-18 – It is reaffirmed that God does see and does hear when the needy are oppressed by the wicked and He does arise to bring justice to the situation.
Prayer Focus: Lord, help me to never give up hope or sight of Your deliverance – even when Your timetable doesn't agree with mine.   Amen.
Notes:




Spiritual Journal:

Week: Four
Day: Sunday morning
Book: Psalms
Chapter: Eleven
Memory Verse: Seven
Principle: When we remember that God is in control and that His intent is to establish righteousness, we don't need to devise our own schemes of deliverance.
Outline:
Verses 1-3 – The psalmist contrasts his trust in the Lord against the uncertainty of those who do not see God's help as present.
Verses 4-6 – The presence of God and His intent to judge unrighteousness is reaffirmed.
Verse 7 – The upright nature of God is verified.
Prayer Focus: Lord, help me always to trust You and not to devise my own plan of escape. Amen.
Notes:




Spiritual Journal:

Week: Four
Day: Sunday evening
Book: Psalms
Chapter: Twelve
Memory Verse: Six
Principle: Even though the visible evidence may not seem to agree, the Word of the Lord is unchangeable and unfailing.
Outline:
 Verses 1-2 – The psalmist calls out for God to help because it seems that good men are being destroyed.
 Verses 3-4 – He cries to God to cut off the ones who speak proudly against God.
 Verses 5-7 – The Lord responds that He will act, and the psalmist testifies that God's words are unfailing.
 Verse 8 – Even though the evil conditions continue, it seems less threatening now that God has spoken.
Prayer Focus: Lord, help me never to doubt Your Word.   Amen.
Notes:



Spiritual Journal:

Week: Five
Day: Saturday
Book: Psalms
Chapter: Thirteen
Memory Verse: Five
Principle: Trusting in the Lord will turn questioning doubts into confident hope.
Outline:

Verses 1-2 – The psalmist expresses his doubt concerning God's timing in his deliverance.

Verses 3-4 – The questioning turns to intercession.

Verses 5-6 – The intercession turns to confident trust and faith-filled praise.

Prayer Focus: Lord, I assume that You permit questions as long as we trust Your answers; help me not to doubt even when I question You.   Amen.

Notes:

Spiritual Journal:

Week: Five
Day: Sunday morning
Book: Psalms
Chapter: Fourteen
Memory Verse: Two
Principle: Even though men ignore God and even deny His existence, He is not ignoring men and He will judge them according to what He has seen.
Outline:
        Verse 1 – The fool denies God's existence and lives wickedly as if God truly does not exist.
        Verses 2-3 – The Lord is, however, watching men and observing that they are perverse in every way.
        Verses 4-6 – The question is asked if the wicked actually are totally without knowledge that God is the avenger of the oppressed.
        Verse 7 – The psalmist utters a plea for deliverance to come.
Prayer Focus: Lord, help me to never – in my thoughts or deeds – ignore or deny You. Amen.
Notes:

Spiritual Journal:

Week: Five
Day: Sunday evening
Book: Psalms
Chapter: Five
Memory Verse: Five
Principle: After repeatedly discussing the wicked who are to be consumed by the Lord, the question is asked as to who will be able to stand in His presence.
Outline:

        Verse 1 – The query is presented.

        Verses 2-5 – The answer is given that it will be the one who is upright in word and deed and does rightly to others – even at his own expense. The summation is that this sort of person will never be dislodged from God's provision.

Prayer Focus: Lord, help me to stand in Your presence and abide in Your temple; that is my greatest desire.   Amen.
Notes:




Spiritual Journal:

Week: Six
Day: Saturday
Book: Psalms
Chapter: Sixteen
Memory Verse: Eleven
Principle: Following the previous psalm which asked who could abide in the presence of the Lord, this psalm celebrates the psalmist's assurance that he will.
Outline:
       Verses 1-2 – The psalmist expresses his confidence in God.
       Verses 3-4 – A contrast between those who serve God and those who serve other gods is painted.
       Verses 5-8 – The psalmist expresses his dedication to God.
       Verses 9-11 – He expresses God's commitment to the believer.
Prayer Focus: Lord, let me walk in the paths of life and experience full joy and Your pleasures forever more.   Amen.
Notes:

Spiritual Journal:

Week: Six

Day: Sunday morning

Book: Psalms

Chapter: Seventeen

Memory Verse: Fifteen

Principle: David proclaims that God has judged his heart and found it pure. Because of this, he has confidence in God's deliverance on his part and judgment against his enemies.

Outline:

        Verses 1-2 – A prayer of vindication is offered.

        Verses 3-9 – The psalmist expresses his confidence in God's preservation based on the purity of his heart.

        Verses 10-13 – The judgment of the wicked is invoked based on their deliberate oppression of others.

        Verses 14-15 – The end of the wicked (that they leave their possessions as an inheritance for their children) and the end of the psalmist (that he will live with God and be transformed into His image) are contrasted.

Prayer Focus: Lord, the New Testament promise is that, when I see You, I will be like You; help me to obtain that promise. Amen.

Notes:

Spiritual Journal:

Week: Six
Day: Sunday evening
Book: Psalms
Chapter: Eighteen
Memory Verse: Twenty-nine
Principle: After his periods of questioning the deliverance – or at least the timing of that deliverance – the psalmist testifies that God has indeed victoriously acted on his behalf.
Outline:

Verses 1-3 – The psalmist proclaims his love for the Lord based on the Lord's character and saving acts.

Verses 4-6 – The psalmist testifies of his critical condition and how he cried out for deliverance in it.

Verses 7-15 – When the Lord moves to deliver, the natural elements respond in trauma.

Verses 16-19 – Not only is the psalmist delivered out of trouble, he is also set into a place of safety.

Verses 20-27 – Deliverance is based on the uprightness of the victim in trouble.

Verses 28-29 – The psalmist recognizes the strengthening he has received from the Lord.

Verses 30-31 – A tribute is offered to God for His qualities of strength.

Verses 32-45 – A testimony of how the Lord has strengthened the psalmist is given.

Verses 46-50 – A reiteration of the Lord's deliverance engenders praise from the psalmist.

Prayer Focus: Lord, You have delivered – and also continue to deliver – me; help me to always praise You for Your faithful and strong deliverance. Amen.
Notes:

Spiritual Journal:

Week: Seven
Day: Saturday
Book: Psalms
Chapter: Nineteen
Memory Verse: Fourteen
Principle: There are three testimonies to the glory of God: the creation (expressed in verses 1-6), the special revelation of Scripture (expressed in verses 7-11), and the personal revelation in the individual (expressed in verses 12-14).
Outline:
  Verses 1-6 – Creation testifies to the majesty of the Lord.
  Verses 7-11 – The divine revelation contained in Scripture is man's source of salvation.
  Verses 12-14 – God's personal inspiration to the individual is necessary for righteous living.
Prayer Focus: Lord, help me to have meditation in my heart and words in my mouth which are acceptable in Thy sight.   Amen.
Notes:




Spiritual Journal:

Week: Seven
Day: Sunday morning
Book: Psalms
Chapter: Twenty
Memory Verse: Seven
Principle: The psalm offers a beautiful progression in the believer's relationship with God: intercession, praise, and testimony – showing God's response to man and his response to God.
Outline:
        Verses 1-4 – The psalmist intercedes for God's mercy.
        Verse 5 – The psalmist offers praise while still expecting God to act – a declaration of faith on the part of the psalmist.
        Verses 6-8 – The psalmist's testimony bears witness to God's intervention.
        Verse 9 – Yet again, the psalmist looks to God to act on his behalf.
Prayer Focus: Lord, help me to trust You, acknowledge You, and thank You in every situation.   Amen.
Notes:




Spiritual Journal:

Week: Seven
Day: Sunday evening
Book: Psalms
Chapter: Twenty-one
Memory Verse: Thirteen
Principle: After closing the previous chapter with a reference to the Lord as King, the psalmist writes this psalm to testify to the fact that the earthly king is dependent upon the heavenly one.
Outline:
> Verses 1-7 – The testimony of how much the earthly king has received from God is given.
> Verses 8-12 – In the previous psalms, the actions of God against the wicked are seen as His acting on behalf of the righteous needy; here, the facts that the wicked are actually God's enemies and that He is acting upon His own behalf are presented.
> Verse 13 – God is exalted.

Prayer Focus: Lord, I do praise You for Your righteous judgments.   Amen.
Notes:


Spiritual Journal:

Week: Eight
Day: Saturday
Book: Psalms
Chapter: Twenty-two
Memory Verse: Twenty-four
Principle: This prophetic psalm, which foretells every detail of the crucifixion, is often misunderstood because it begins with a proclamation that the Lord has forsaken His Christ. However, verse 24 clarifies that – regardless of the initial appearance – God has not turned His back on Christ.
Outline:
Verses 1-18 – The crucifixion is prophesied in detail, giving such minute points as the ridicule Christ endured, His thirsting, the piercing of His hands and feet, and the gambling for His garments.
Verses 19-21 – A prayer for deliverance is punctuated with a testimony that God has answered.
Verses 22-26 – Praise for deliverance is offered.
Verses 27-31 – Salvation for the gentiles and for all future generations will be the conclusion of the crucifixion plan.
Prayer Focus: Lord, I am amazed at how You can and do tell the future in such detail in advance. Help me to genuinely trust that You really do hold the future in Your hand. Amen.
Notes:

Spiritual Journal:

Week: Eight

Day: Sunday morning

Book: Psalms

Chapter: Twenty-three

Memory Verse: One

Principle: The historical setting of this psalm is that David penned it while being chased by King Saul who was determined to kill him. What a proclamation of confidence in God during a time of real danger!

Outline:

Verses 1-4 – David draws on his experience as a shepherd to describe the care which the Lord demonstrates for His beloved.

Verses 5-6 – Even in the sight of his enemies, God's provision and blessings are bestowed on the trusting believer.

Prayer Focus: Lord, help me to realize that my heart can abide in Your green pastures even when my physical man is in the valley of the shadow of death. Amen.

Notes:

Spiritual Journal:

Week: Eight
Day: Sunday evening
Book: Psalms
Chapter: Twenty-four
Memory Verse: Ten
Principle: In a previous chapter, the psalmist addressed the issue of being permitted to enter into the presence of the Lord. Here, he clarifies that the only one genuinely qualified is the Messiah Himself.
Outline:
> Verses 1-2 – The psalmist affirms that all the earth and its inhabitants belong to the Lord.
>
> Verses 3-6 – The psalmist asks the question and then answers his own question concerning the qualifications for someone to enter into the presence of such a God.
>
> Verses 7-10 – A proclamation is made for the portals of heaven to prepare themselves for the entry of the one who is qualified to come in – the Messiah.

Prayer Focus: Lord, I rejoice in the ascent of the Messiah Jesus into the holy hill of God. But even more, I am awed by the New Testament invitation for me as a believer to sit with Him in those heavenly places. Amen
Notes:




Spiritual Journal:

Week: Nine
Day: Saturday
Book: Psalms
Chapter: Twenty-five
Memory Verse: Twenty-one

Principle: This psalm is a proclamation of the psalmist's dependence upon God and a request for God to avenge him due to his reliance upon and obedience to the Lord. He admits that his sin debt exceeds his own resources and calls on God for pardon based simply upon God's own character and reputation.

Outline:

Verses 1-4 – The psalmist draws attention to the trust he has placed in the Lord and requests that God honor this dependency.

Verses 5-11 – Demonstrating a shift in reasoning, the psalmist calls upon God's own nature (rather than the actions of man) as the foundation for God's responsiveness to man.

Verses 12-15 – The believer's fear (or reverent respect) of the Lord is presented as another plank in the platform upon which God's care for man stands.

Verses 16-21 – The psalmist reiterates his request for God's intervention based upon his trust in the Lord; this time, he adds another reason for expecting God's response: the desolation and affliction he is suffering.

Verse 22 – The psalmist's prayer is expanded to include the whole nation as well as himself individually.

Prayer Focus: Lord, the Living Bible translates verse 21 with the term "bodyguards" to refer to integrity and uprightness. Help me to always keep my bodyguards on duty. Amen.

Notes:

Spiritual Journal:

Week: Nine
Day: Sunday morning
Book: Psalms
Chapter: Twenty-six
Memory Verse: One

Principle: Some believers may have a "sin complex" and call themselves "sinners saved by grace," but the psalmist boldly proclaimed his righteousness and right standing with the Lord.  We are told to be perfect even as God Himself is perfect – a command which most of us interpret as a target to shoot for rather than an actual attainable goal.  Perhaps this psalm and the testimony of Job, which it seems to echo, could help us rethink such a stance.

Outline:
Verses 1-2 – The psalmist invites the Lord to examine his life and see that it is perfect.
Verses 3-8 – He proclaims his past and present purity and his intentions for future continuance.
Verses 9-12 – He expresses his anticipation of God's preservation as a return for his uprightness.

Prayer Focus: Lord, I want to be careful not to think more highly of myself than I ought to think, nor do I want to assume that any righteousness I have demonstrated is a result of my own goodness; but I do desire to have a spotless testimony which I can proclaim unashamedly.  Amen.

Notes:

Spiritual Journal:

Week: Nine

Day: Sunday evening

Book: Psalms

Chapter: Twenty-seven

Memory Verse: One

Principle: Affirmation, intercession, and testimony blend together in this chapter to paint a vivid picture of the relationship between the psalmist and his deliverer.

Outline:

> Verses 1-3 – The psalmist begins by affirming God's action on his behalf.
>
> Verses 4-6 – Next, he declares an affirmation of his determination to live worthy of the Lord's intervention in his life.
>
> Verses 7-12 – The next focus of attention is intercession for God to act on his behalf, showing that the mercies of the Lord are not to be taken for granted and assumed to be automatic.
>
> Verses 13-14 – The psalmist testifies of how the Lord has acted to deliver him and adds that it happened in the "land of the living" – not in the "sweet by and by."

Prayer Focus: Lord, as I read this psalm, I see a pattern which seems to have developed as the psalmist wrote: in one chapter, he said that the Messiah would ascend to the holy hill of God; next, he wrote that he (as a human) was righteous; now, he writes that the Lord is his light and salvation and that his greatest desire is to dwell in the Lord's house. My prayer is that I might truly know the Lord as my salvation so that I can be perfect and enter into the heavenly places with Him as he ascends. Amen.

Notes:

Spiritual Journal:

Week: Ten
Day: Saturday
Book: Psalms
Chapter: Twenty-eight
Memory Verse: Seven
Principle: This chapter illustrates the prayer of faith that produces results in that it begins with a faith statement about the delivering qualities of God followed by intercession which immediately breaks forth into a jubilant proclamation of assurance in God's answer.

Outline:

Verse 1 – The psalmist initiates his petition with the proclamation that God is his rock (strength and protection).

Verses 2-3 – He entreats God for intervention and deliverance.

Verses 4-5 – He further petitions God to bring justice upon his enemies.

Verses 6-7 – An immediate proclamation of victory is a testimony to the faith which accompanied the psalmist's supplication.

Verses 8-9 – The victory expands beyond the individual believer to include the entire nation.

Prayer Focus: Lord, help me to learn to pray in faith and to not doubt in my heart so that I will have whatsoever I proclaim in my prayers.   Amen.

Notes:

Spiritual Journal:

Week: Ten

Day: Sunday morning

Book: Psalms

Chapter: Twenty-nine

Memory Verse: Two

Principle: The majesty of the Lord revealed in nature demands worship and recognition of His strength.

Outline:

Verses 1-2 – In anticipation of the qualities to be enumerated in the following verses, the psalmist demands that adequate praise and honor be given to the Lord.

Verses 3-8 – The awesome power of the voice of the Lord is portrayed in what seems to be a comparison to an earthquake.

Verse 9 – In an expression reminiscent of the creation story where God spoke everything into being, the voice of the Lord is attributed with the quality to give life and the proclamation is made that the entire created order (those in His temple of creation) testifies of His glory.

Verses 10-11 – Not only does the Lord reign in dominion, He also uses His dominion for the benefit of His people.

Prayer Focus: Lord, I stand amazed at Your magnificent power in the creation, but I am even more awestruck at the glory of Your redemptive power.   Amen.

Notes:

Spiritual Journal:

Week: Ten
Day: Sunday evening
Book: Psalms
Chapter: Thirty
Memory Verse: Eleven
Principle: Just as the former psalm magnified the glory of God in creation, this one exalts the redemptive acts of the Lord.
Outline:
  Verses 1-3 – The psalmist determines to proclaim the greatness of God who has delivered him.
  Verses 4-5 – He enlists all saints to join him in his praise to the Lord.
  Verses 6-7 – God has not only delivered the psalmist, He has established him in unshakable security.
  Verses 8-10 – The psalmist illustrates how simple an intercession he had to offer to obtain the Lord's assistance.
  Verses 11-12 – He gives testimony of and offers thanks for the Lord's complete reversal of his situation.
Prayer Focus: Lord, You have indeed delivered me from the kingdom of darkness and translated me into the kingdom of Your dear Son.  For this, I praise You and give You thanks.  Amen.
Notes:

Spiritual Journal:

Week: Eleven
Day: Saturday
Book: Psalms
Chapter: Thirty-one
Memory Verse: Twenty-four
Principle: Trusting God results in receiving deliverance at His hand.
Outline:

       Verses 1-8 – Every action of confident trust by the psalmist results in a greater action of deliverance by the Lord.

       Verses 9-13 – The psalmist describes his desperate condition.

       Verses 14-18 – Beginning with the word "but," the psalmist indicates that the condition is going to change as he calls upon the Lord to act.

       Verses 19-24 – He reiterates that it is the Lord's nature and intent to deliver those who trust in Him. Even when we are impatient and evaluate our condition before He intervenes, we can be assured that He is going to act when we place our hope in him.

Prayer Focus: Lord, help me not to lose my confident trust in You or become impatient as I wait for Your deliverance. Amen.

Notes:

Spiritual Journal:

Week: Eleven
Day: Sunday morning
Book: Psalms
Chapter: Thirty-two
Memory Verse: Seven
Principle: When confession of any transgressions accompanies the cry for deliverance, God responds.
Outline:

       Verses 1-2 – A proclamation of the blessing of forgiveness is given.

       Verses 3-4 – A description of the dread of those who have not repented is declared.

       Verses 5-7 – The confident trust of the penitent sinner is the summation of the movement of the psalm up to this point.

       Verses 8-10 – The Lord Himself speaks and proclaims that He will instruct His people if they will not be too stubborn to listen.

       Verse 11 – An exclamation of the praiseworthiness of God punctuates the psalm.

Prayer Focus: Lord, help me to be willing to repent so that You can deal mightily on my behalf. Amen.
Notes:

Spiritual Journal:

Week: Eleven
Day: Sunday evening
Book: Psalms
Chapter: Thirty-three
Memory Verse: Twelve
Principle: The Lord whose word was powerful enough to establish the earth is also a trustworthy protector for any nation or individual.
Outline:

> Verses 1-3 – The righteous are commanded to praise the Lord.
> Verses 4-7 – The mighty words and works of the Lord are magnified.
> Verse 8 – Reverential fear of the Lord is required from all the earth.
> Verses 9-11 – The sovereignty of the Lord is portrayed.
> Verse 12 – The blessedness of the nation which follows the Lord is declared.
> Verses 13-17 – The sovereignty of the Lord is again emphasized.
> Verses 18-22 – The declaration of the Lord's delivering nature is followed by a statement of the psalmist's dependence upon that deliverance and a prayer for that deliverance.

Prayer Focus: Lord, help me and my nation as a whole to obtain the blessedness that is only available through trusting and obeying You.   Amen.
Notes:




Spiritual Journal:

Week: Twelve
Day: Saturday
Book: Psalms
Chapter: Thirty-four
Memory Verse: Seventeen
Principle: Today's memory verse expresses the theme or principle of this psalm; the Lord
   is a deliverer to those who will trust Him to be.
Outline:
    Verses 1-3 – The psalmist declares his praise for the Lord and invites others to
     join him.
    Verses 4-6 – He gives his testimony of the Lord's deliverance.
    Verses 7-10 – The testimony is expanded to encompass all who will trust in the
     Lord.
    Verses 11-14 – The psalmist offers to instruct others in how to trust in God.
    Verses 15-22 – The ever-active role of the Lord in delivering the righteous and
     judging the unrighteous is portrayed.
Prayer Focus: Lord, sometimes it's just too hard for me as a human to trust You to deliver
   me out of all my troubles; help me to trust You in every situation.   Amen.
Notes:




Spiritual Journal:

Week: Twelve
Day: Sunday morning
Book: Psalms
Chapter: Thirty-five
Memory Verse: Twenty-seven
Principle: To vindicate the righteous, judgment must be executed against the wicked; however, it is noteworthy that the psalmist testifies of his loving care toward his enemies before he finally resorts to his plea for judgment.
Outline:

        Verses 1-8 – The psalmist calls upon the Lord to judge his enemies.

        Verses 9-10 – He anticipates rejoicing as a result of the Lord's intervention.

        Verses 11-16 – The psalmist testifies of his righteous actions and attitude toward his enemy even though the enemy had treated him so despitefully.

        Verses 17-26 – He prays for vindication.

        Verses 27-28 – He calls for joyous praise and testimony as a result of the Lord's intervention.

Prayer Focus: Lord, help me to be able to love my enemy and pray for him as Jesus taught but to also love righteousness enough to trust You to display Your vengeance when necessary.   Amen.
Notes:

Spiritual Journal:

Week: Twelve

Day: Sunday evening

Book: Psalms

Chapter: Thirty-six

Memory Verse: Nine

Principle: The theme of this psalm is one that is found often in the Bible, yet it bears constant repeating: the wicked will be destroyed and the righteous will be blessed.

Outline:

        Verses 1-4 – The wicked heart of the unrighteous is described.

        Verses 5-9 – The magnitude of the Lord's blessing and mercy for the righteous is described.

        Verses 10-11 – The psalmist intercedes for the blessings of the Lord to be made continually available to him.

        Verse 12 – The wicked are cast down without hope of rising again.

Prayer Focus: Lord, the difference between the lives and the destinies of the righteous and the wicked is so graphically obvious; help me to never forget and fall into the camp of the wicked. Amen.

Notes:

Spiritual Journal:

Week: Thirteen
Day: Saturday
Book: Psalms
Chapter: Thirty-seven
Memory Verse: Sixteen
Principle: When the fate of the wicked and the destiny of the righteous are compared, God's people should have no reason to fret or doubt that He will take care of them.
Outline:

Verses 1-22 – The psalmist encourages the righteous to continue to trust God and to stop being concerned about the wicked because the righteous will soon be established and the wicked destroyed.

Verses 23-40 – The psalmist reiterates the promise that the Lord is working in and for the righteous so that they will be established when the wicked are judged.

Prayer Focus: Lord, help me to never fret or worry when the wicked seem to be in control. Help me to always keep my eyes on what You are doing rather than what my enemy has seemingly accomplished. Amen.
Notes:

Spiritual Journal:

Week: Thirteen
Day: Sunday morning
Book: Psalms
Chapter: Thirty-eight
Memory Verse: Twenty-one
Principle: Deep intercession and travail of soul are portrayed in this psalm.
Outline:

Verses 1-10 – The psalmist graphically illustrates his anguish of soul and the intensity of his prayers.

Verses 11-20 – The psalmist's vulnerable and suffering position is described.

Verses 21-22 – He concludes with a genuine plea for God's intervention.

Prayer Focus: Lord, help me to never look at my circumstances but to rather look only upon You.   Amen.

Notes:

Spiritual Journal:

Week: Thirteen
Day: Sunday evening
Book: Psalms
Chapter: Thirty-nine
Memory Verse: Four
Principle: The brevity of life and the difficulties encountered in it can drive us to a desperate dependence upon the Lord.
Outline:

Verses 1-3 – The psalmist testifies to his determination to guard his tongue even while experiencing anguish of heart.

Verses 4-7 – In order to keep proper perspective on his life, the psalmist asks the Lord to allow him to realize how brief life is and how impermanent the achievements of life are.

Verses 8-11 – He prays that the Lord's chastisement be removed from him.

Verses 12-13 – He ends his intercession with a plea for restoration.

Prayer Focus: Lord, help me to always keep this fleeting life in proper perspective to the endlessness of eternity.   Amen.

Notes:

Spiritual Journal:

Week: Fourteen
Day: Saturday
Book: Psalms
Chapter: Forty
Memory Verse: Five
Principle: We can have confidence in our prayers for a speedy deliverance just as the psalmist did if our prayers are based on the same two great pillars: our testimony of previous deliverance and our obedience to the Lord's will.
Outline:

    Verses 1-4 – The psalmist's testimony verifies that trusting God does result in deliverance.

    Verse 5 – The blessings of the Lord are too numerous to count.

    Verses 6-10 – The psalmist confirms that he has followed the Lord's will – not rituals but witness.

    Verses 11-17 – The intercession for a speedy deliverance ends with an affirmation of confidence.

Prayer Focus: Lord, help me to always live a life which will result in confidence when I pray. Amen.
Notes:

Spiritual Journal:

Week: Fourteen
Day: Sunday morning
Book: Psalms
Chapter: Forty-one
Memory Verse: One
Principle: The conflicts of the present world are overcome through the mercies of the Lord, which is activated by the believer's integrity and charity toward the poor.
Outline:
Verses 1-3 – Blessings are promised to those who show loving mercy to the poor.
Verses 4-9 – The predicament in which the psalmist finds himself includes not only hostility from his known enemies but also from his presumed friends.
Verses 10-13 – God is to be praised for His deliverance of the psalmist.
Prayer Focus: Lord, I never want to fail to receive Your deliverance, so help me to never fail to bless the poor and guard my integrity. Amen.
Notes:




Spiritual Journal:

Week: Fourteen
Day: Sunday evening
Book: Psalms
Chapter: Forty-two
Memory Verse: One
Principle: To comprehend the fullness of this passage, we must first understand the principle of the three-part composition of the human being. I Thessalonians 5:23 teaches us that man consists of a body, a soul, and a spirit. Each of these parts has a specific function: the body communicates with the environment around us, the soul communicates with people, and the spirit communicates with God. In this passage, the psalmist's soul is distressed as it reviews his circumstances; but the spirit, having reviewed his spiritual situation, speaks encouragement to him.

Outline:
>
> Verses 1-2 – The psalmist confirms that his soulical part is in desperate need of communication with God.
>
> Verses 3-4 – He declares that his desperate condition has caused his soul to be poured out or distressed.
>
> Verses 5-11 – The spirit encourages the soul that there is no reason to be cast down when considering all the ways in which the Lord will deliver and strengthen the believer.

Prayer Focus: Lord, help me to always live in my spirit rather than to be dominated by the unrenewed soul or the carnal flesh.

Notes:

Spiritual Journal:

Week: Fifteen
Day: Saturday
Book: Psalms
Chapter: Forty-three
Memory Verse: Five
Principle: Realizing that God is our defense gives us reason to worship and be encouraged.
Outline:

Verse 1 – The psalmist prays for the Lord to judge him and to plead his case.

Verse 2 – He reminds himself that the Lord is his strength and there is, therefore, no reason to be distressed.

Verses 3-4 – He asked for the Lord to lead him out of danger and promises that he will follow into the Temple to praise the Lord.

Verse 5 – The psalmist's spirit repeats his previous inquiry to the soul as to why he has allowed himself to be distressed when he could be trusting in the Lord.

Prayer Focus: Lord, help me to never let my doubting soul dominate over my trusting spirit.   Amen.

Notes:

Spiritual Journal:

Week: Fifteen
Day: Sunday morning
Book: Psalms
Chapter: Forty-four
Memory Verse: Eight
Principle: Even when it looks as if there is no way out, we must not stop praising the Lord and testifying of His goodness.
Outline:

Verses 1-3 – The psalmist recounts the testimonies he has heard of his God.

Verses 4-8 – He boasts of the Lord's great qualities and acts.

Verses 9-16 – The psalmist describes his desperate plight and wonders why God has not intervened.

Verses 17-22 – He proclaims his continued trust in and dependence upon the Lord regardless of his condition.

Verses 23-26 – He summons the Lord to act on his behalf.

Prayer Focus: Lord, help me to always keep my confidence in You even when the circumstances would tell me not to.   Amen.

Notes:

Spiritual Journal:

Week: Fifteen
Day: Sunday evening
Book: Psalms
Chapter: Forty-five
Memory Verse: Seven
Principle: Just as Christ the Messianic King is revealed as glorious, the church His bride is portrayed as radiant.
Outline:
  Verses 1-5 – The king is described in splendor and victory as blessed by God.
  Verses 6-8 – As he continues to speak of the blessings of God upon the king, the psalmist also speaks of the king as God – showing that the king he is describing is the Messiah.
  Verses 9-16 – The church is described as the glorious bride of the King.
  Verse 17 – The fact that the king will be praised for all generations is an obvious reference to the truth that he is not just a human ruler.
Prayer Focus: Lord, I want to be counted worthy of being included as part of the glorious church which is bride to the majestic King.
Notes:




Spiritual Journal:

Week: Sixteen
Day: Saturday
Book: Psalms
Chapter: Forty-six
Memory Verse: Ten
Principle: It is important for us to learn to stand still and let God manifest Himself in the
    midst of our conflicts because He is ready to act when we cease to interfere.
Outline:
        Verses 1-3 – Because God is our refuge, there is no reason to fear regardless of
            the devastation we encounter.
        Verses 4-7 – The presence of God in the midst of His people brings joy and
            security.
        Verses 8-11 – If we will but be still and recognize the Lord's presence, we will see
            that He will be exalted as He makes conflicts to cease and destroys the
            implements of war.
Prayer Focus: Lord, help me to really recognize You as my refuge to the point that I can
    actually be still in the presence of conflict while You do Your work of making the
    war to cease and making glad the hearts of the city of God.   Amen.
Notes:

Spiritual Journal:

Week: Sixteen
Day: Sunday morning
Book: Psalms
Chapter: Forty-seven
Memory Verse: One
Principle: The lesson of this chapter is the same one presented in Second Chronicles chapter twenty where we read the story of how Jehoshaphat won a victory through praise: the confidence to praise God for a victory even before it is manifest is the kind of faith that activates God on our behalf.
Outline:
Verses 1-5 – The psalmist calls for praise because God will vindicate His people.
Verses 6-9 – He calls for praise because of God's reigning position of authority.
Prayer Focus: Lord, there are conflicts which are not yet resolved in my life, but – as an act of faith – I praise You in advance for the victory in every one of them! Amen.
Notes:

Spiritual Journal:

Week: Sixteen
Day: Sunday evening
Book: Psalms
Chapter: Forty-eight
Memory Verse: One
Principle: Just as the presence of God in Jerusalem was considered to be the defense of the city, His presence in our lives is also our strength and security.
Outline:
> Verses 1-3 – The location of Jerusalem with the natural defense of deep canyons on three sides and the belief that God Himself sat as the blockade on the fourth boundary gave the people inside the city a sense of safety.
>
> Verses 4-8 – The nations which would have attacked gave up their plans in fear.
>
> Verses 9-14 – The psalmist encourages the people to meditate on the Lord's presence and praise Him for His protection.

Prayer Focus: Lord, help me to always see that You are there defending and guarding my very habitation. Amen.
Notes:

Spiritual Journal:

Week: Seventeen
Day: Saturday
Book: Psalms
Chapter: Forty-nine
Memory Verse: Three
Principle: It doesn't matter how much money or intelligence a person may have; his position with God is not based on any of this physical qualities.
Outline:

Verses 1-4 – The psalmist invites everyone to hear his psalm which will reveal some of the secrets of the universe.

Verses 5-9 – He explains that wealth is not the key to redemption.

Verses 10-13 – He explains that the wise man and the foolish man alike are destined to death and being forgotten.

Verses 14-15 – The righteous has a better promise and a guaranteed future.

Verses 16-19 – The wealth of men will not go with them at death.

Verse 20 – Although man is honored as the crown of creation, if he does not understand his place, he is nothing more than a beast.

Prayer Focus: Lord, the sayings of this passage are called "dark"; help me to see the light in them and to live by their revelation. Amen.

Notes:

Spiritual Journal:

Week: Seventeen
Day: Sunday morning
Book: Psalms
Chapter: Fifty
Memory Verse: Twenty-three
Principle: In this psalm, God demonstrates that He does not need man's offerings; rather, He desires man's worship and obedience.
Outline:

> Verses 1-6 – The Lord calls the human race to trial concerning man's obligations to God.
>
> Verses 7-13 – The Lord details His arguments that He does not need man's sacrifices.
>
> Verses 14-15 – The sacrifice which God approves of and responds to is the offering of praise.
>
> Verses 16-22 – The sinner's lips have been used for evil; therefore, God will not respond when he calls.
>
> Verse 23 – God's salvation is for the one who praises God and carefully directs his conversation.

Prayer Focus: Lord, I want to offer You a righteous life and a pure tongue as a sacrifice You can accept. Amen.
Notes:

Spiritual Journal:

Week: Seventeen
Day: Sunday evening
Book: Psalms
Chapter: Fifty-one
Memory Verse: Ten
Principle: This psalm was the repentance prayer which David prayed after he was confronted concerning the murder of Uriah and adultery with his wife. Notice that he never speaks of these sins in specific but focuses on the sin nature in his heart which was the core of the problems which were eventually manifest in his physical actions.
Outline:
    Verses 1-2 – The psalmist begs for mercy.
    Verses 3-6 – He acknowledges his sinfulness and recognizes that his problem is between himself and God, not with Bathsheba or Uriah.
    Verses 7-15 – David delineates the positive responses for each of the restorative actions he is expecting from God:
        a) Purge...I will be clean
        b) Wash...I will be white
        c) Make me hear joy...my bones will rejoice
        d) Hide from my sin, blot out my iniquities, create a clean heart, renew a right spirit, don't cast me away, don't take away Your spirit, restore, uphold...I will teach sinners and they will be converted
        e) Deliver...I will sing
        f) Open my lips...I will praise
    Verses 16-19 – Having explained that the real sacrifice the Lord desires is praise backed by a holy life, the psalmist further clarifies that God does accept Temple worship and offerings from His righteous people.
Prayer Focus: Lord, help me to be ready to repent and receive Your restoration for all my sinful acts but more importantly for the sinful heart which gives birth to them. Amen.
Notes:




Spiritual Journal:

Week: Eighteen
Day: Saturday
Book: Psalms
Chapter: Fifty-two
Memory Verse: Eight
Principle: As has been illustrated in a number of psalms already, this chapter compares the destruction of the wicked and the preservation of the righteous.
Outline:
       Verses 1-4 – The evil words and intents of the wicked are described.
       Verse 5 – God's judgment against such wickedness is described.
       Verses 6-7 – The righteous person's accusations against the wicked are illustrated.
       Verses 8-9 – The assurance of the upright is contrasted against the destruction of the wicked.
Prayer Focus: Lord, help me to always trust in You so that I can be like that green olive tree in Your house forever.   Amen.
Notes:


Spiritual Journal:

Week: Eighteen
Day: Sunday morning
Book: Psalms
Chapter: Fifty-three
Memory Verse: One
Principle: The only solution for man's depravity is that the Messiah would appear.
Outline:

Verses 1-5 – The total depravity of the entire human race and God's judgment upon man are depicted.

Verse 6 – The wickedness of man and God's judgment upon that wickedness sets the stage for the psalmist's plea that the Messiah would be revealed.

Prayer Focus: Lord, my prayer today echoes the closing words of the book of Revelation, "Even so, come, Lord Jesus."   Amen.

Notes:

Spiritual Journal:

Week: Eighteen
Day: Sunday evening
Book: Psalms
Chapter: Fifty-four
Memory Verse: Four
Principle: This psalm is a declaration of confidence in God's protection.   It was written at a point in Saul's pursuit of David when David's whereabouts had been revealed and it seemed that Saul would be able to capture and kill him.
Outline:
        Verses 1-3 – The psalmist prays for protection.
        Verses 4-5 – He declares his confidence that God will deliver him.
        Verses 6-7 – He looks forward to the opportunity to praise and worship God after his deliverance.
Prayer Focus: Lord, help me to always have the same kind of confident trust in You as David demonstrated in this psalm.   Amen.
Notes:

Spiritual Journal:

Week: Nineteen
Day: Saturday
Book: Psalms
Chapter: Fifty-five
Memory Verse: Seventeen
Principle: This psalm depicts the despair of soul David experienced when his trusted counselors turned traitor during Absalom's revolt. From his experience, we can learn how the Lord can protect us not only from our enemies, but also from our supposed friends.
Outline:
> Verses 1-5 – David's appeal to the Lord expresses his extreme anguish at this moment.
>
> Verses 6-8 – Psychologists describe the reactions to danger as "fight or flight" reflexes. In this encounter with a traitor, David exhibits the flight response; whereas, he has always demonstrated the fight response when confronted by known enemies.
>
> Verses 9-11 – He calls on God to punish his opponents.
>
> Verses 12-14 – He expresses his distress in the betrayal by the traitor.
>
> Verses 15-19 – The psalmist expects God to judge the enemy and preserve the righteous.
>
> Verses 20-21 – The psalmist delineates the sins of his betrayer.
>
> Verses 22-23 – He encourages others to trust in the Lord to execute justice.

Prayer Focus: Lord, help me to know my true friends and to discern the Judases who may invade my life. Amen.
Notes:

Spiritual Journal:

Week: Nineteen
Day: Sunday morning
Book: Psalms
Chapter: Fifty-six
Memory Verse: Eleven
Principle: This psalm, which was written when David was taken by the Philistines, declares that there were two different designs placed on his life: the design of man to destroy him and the plan of God to protect and restore him. When we trust God, His design is always triumphant.
Outline:
        Verses 1-2 – The psalmist pleas for mercy from God in light of the enemy's desire to destroy him.
        Verses 3-4 – Trusting in God results in fearlessness and praise.
        Verses 5-7 – The enemy's evil plan is described.
        Verses 8-11 – The psalmist is fearless and full of praise because God takes special note of and care for him.
        Verses 12-13 – Victorious praise is the conclusion of the matter.
Prayer Focus: Lord, help me never to fear men but rather to trust You. Amen.
Notes:

Spiritual Journal:

Week: Nineteen
Day: Sunday evening
Book: Psalms
Chapter: Fifty-seven
Memory Verse: Seven
Principle: This psalm, which was written while David was hiding from King Saul, expresses the same theme as the previous chapter. Here, two psalms written under two different situations demonstrate that the same God is our deliverer – no matter what the circumstance.
Outline:

> Verses 1-4 – The psalmist calls for the Lord to deliver him in his desperate situation.
> Verses 5-6 – He praises God that He has caused his enemies to be caught in their own trap.
> Verses 7-11 – He determines to praise the Lord for his deliverance.

Prayer Focus: Lord, I do praise You for Your continued deliverance from every situation in which I am entrapped. Amen.
Notes:

Spiritual Journal:

Week: Twenty
Day: Saturday
Book: Psalms
Chapter: Fifty-eight
Memory Verse: Eleven
Principle: The wicked will be judged and the righteous established.
Outline:

        Verses 1-8 – The wickedness of the psalmist's enemies is described in the graphic terminology of a serpent; their demise is illustrated with the dissolving of a snail. The deliberate contrast between a slug with an adder depicts the magnitude of God's vengeance against them.

        Verses 9-11 – The reward of the righteous is God's speedy and complete deliverance.

Prayer Focus: Lord, help me to never exalt myself as a cobra only to find myself reduced to a slug. Amen.
Notes:

Spiritual Journal:

Week: Twenty
Day: Sunday morning
Book: Psalms
Chapter: Fifty-nine
Memory Verse: Sixteen
Principle: This chapter repeats the theme of several chapters within this section of the Psalms: the wicked are judged and the righteous are preserved. One added element in this psalm is that their unjustified accusations against the righteous is the key element for vengeance against the wicked.
Outline:
Verses 1-7 – The psalmist petitions the Lord to judge the wicked for their unfounded attacks against him.
Verses 8-10 – He reaffirms his confidence in the deliverance of the Lord.
Verses 11-15 – Retribution to be taken against the wicked is delineated. One interesting note is the play on words concerning the dog sounds the enemy made. In verse 6, they were ferocious sounds of an angry beast threatening any intruders; here, they are the whisperings of a starving animal scavenging for food.
Verses 16-17 – The psalm ends with a song of praise to the deliverer.
Prayer Focus: Lord, thank you for preserving me while You reveal my opponents for the "dirty dogs" they are. Amen.
Notes:

Spiritual Journal:

Week: Twenty
Day: Sunday evening
Book: Psalms
Chapter: Sixty
Memory Verse: Twelve
Principle: The progression of the psalm – from defeat and the feeling of having been abandoned by God to the final statement in the concluding verse – shows the change that takes place when we learn to trust God.
Outline:
        Verses 1-5 – The desperate condition of the psalmist is portrayed.
        Verses 6-8 – The Lord's authority over the nations is declared.
        Verses 9-10 – The psalmist expresses his dependence upon the Lord.
        Verses 11-12 – The assurance of victorious triumph is the result of trusting in God.
Prayer Focus: Lord, I want to be known as a man who does valiantly through my confidence in You. Amen.
Notes:



Spiritual Journal:

Week: Twenty-one
Day: Saturday
Book: Psalms
Chapter: Sixty-one
Memory Verse: Four
Principle: There is safety and protection in the presence of the Lord.
Outline:

> Verses 1-2 – The psalmist determines that he will call upon the Lord no matter where he is or what situation he finds himself in.
>
> Verses 3-7 – The psalmist determines to abide in the presence of the Lord because it is his place of sanctuary and refuge.
>
> Verse 8 – Praise and thanksgiving offerings are in order upon the Lord's deliverance.

Prayer Focus: Lord, I do seek the protection of Your presence, but most of all I seek Your presence because I desire to be with You.   Amen.
Notes:

Spiritual Journal:

Week: Twenty-one
Day: Sunday morning
Book: Psalms
Chapter: Sixty-two
Memory Verse: Seven
Principle: There is no source of meaning, purpose, or power outside God Himself.
Outline:

> Verses 1-2 – The psalmist identifies God as his only salvation, defense, and protection.
>
> Verses 3-4 – The precarious position and the unstable future of the accuser of the righteous are illustrated with a wall and a tower that are ready to collapse.
>
> Verses 5-7 – The psalmist reminds himself that there is no salvation other than the Lord.
>
> Verse 8 – He expands his exhortation to trust in the Lord alone to all people.
>
> Verse 9 – Having portrayed the solidity of the Lord, the psalmist turns to the frailty of man by saying that men of low degree are nothing and that men of high degree are even less.
>
> Verses 10-11 – Men view wealth and position as power or authority, but the psalmist proclaims that God had repeatedly declared that He alone has power.
>
> Verse 12 – The psalmist ends the section with a plea for much-needed mercy.

Prayer Focus: Lord, help me to always realize that all else will fail and that I must trust in Your power which is available through Your mercy.   Amen.

Notes:

Spiritual Journal:

Week: Twenty-one
Day: Sunday evening
Book: Psalms
Chapter: Sixty-three
Memory Verse: One
Principle: A desire to know and experience God brings the believer into the presence and
protection of God.
Outline:
Verses 1-8 – The psalmist expresses his adamant desire for the presence of God.
He proclaims his confidence in the sheltering provision of the Lord as the
result of his pursuit of God's presence.
Verses 9-11 – In contrast to the provision which the righteous king expects from
the Lord, his enemies are to be utterly decimated.
Prayer Focus: Lord, help me to genuinely seek You, not just Your protection.   Amen.
Notes:

Spiritual Journal:

Week: Twenty-two
Day: Saturday
Book: Psalms
Chapter: Sixty-four
Memory Verse: Ten
Principle: The New Testament expresses the principle in the words of reaping what you
      sow; the modern vernacular expresses it in terms of having a dose of your own
      medicine; this psalm declares that the wicked will be shot at by the bow of God if
      they aim their bows at God's beloved.
Outline:
      Verses 1-6 – The psalmist describes the accusations of his enemies as bows and
          arrows aimed at Him.
      Verses 7-8 – God will fight against the psalmist's enemies with the arrows of His
          mouth and cause them to be inflicted by their own attacks. The
          terminology is suggestive of the picture of the conquering Christ in
          Revelation who destroys His enemies with the sword of His mouth.
      Verses 9-10 – The result will be the declaration of the works of God.
Prayer Focus: Lord, each time I am tempted to criticize or gossip, help me to remember
      that what goes around is what will come around and that every tongue which rises
      up in accusations will be condemned.   Amen.
Notes:

Spiritual Journal:

Week: Twenty-two

Day: Sunday morning

Book: Psalms

Chapter: Sixty-five

Memory Verse: One

Principle: After several psalms in which the Lord is portrayed as victorious yet militant in nature, this psalm paints the picture of God's greatness on the canvas of His creation.

Outline:

Verses 1-4 – God is worthy of praise because of His salvation qualities which are defined in the New Testament as justification, redemption, and adoption.

Verses 5-13 – His care for and control of the created order are described as "terrible things" (meaning "awe-inspiring") which engender confidence in those who pray to Him.

Prayer Focus: Lord, in the book of Romans, Paul teaches that there is enough of Your nature expressed in the universe around us for man to have a revelation of You. Help me to see Your fingerprint and portrait in the world You have created. Amen.

Notes:

Spiritual Journal:

Week: Twenty-two
Day: Sunday evening
Book: Psalms
Chapter: Sixty-six
Memory Verse: One
Principle: After having described the work of God in creation as "terrible" (awe-inspiring), the psalmist uses the same terminology to speak of the revelation of God which we receive when He answers prayer. In other words, creation and redemption are both expressions of the nature of our Lord.
Outline:
Verses 1-4 – The earth is required to sing and worship God as a result of the revelation to be expressed in the psalm.
Verses 5-12 – The colossal deliverance of the Israelites through the Red Sea and His ongoing deliverance of His children warrants praise and blessing.
Verses 13-15 – The psalmist promises to make offerings and perform vows of thanksgiving for the Lord's deliverance.
Verses 16-20 – He invites others to come hear his testimony of and teaching concerning God's ability and activity in answering prayer.
Prayer Focus: Lord, Jews often refer to you simply as "He who answers prayer." Help me to keep that revelation foremost in my own thinking. Amen.
Notes:


Spiritual Journal:

Week: Twenty-three
Day: Saturday
Book: Psalms
Chapter: Sixty-seven
Memory Verse: Seven

Principle: The covenant given to the Jewish people through Abraham and codified through Moses promised that they would be blessed so that they would be a proof to the rest of the world that theirs was the true God who would dwell with His people and cause them to prosper. This psalm uses the Jewish terminology of "people" for the Jews and "nations" for the gentiles to express the idea that the gentiles will receive the Lord once the Jews are properly blessed as a testimony before them.

Outline:
> Verses 1-2 – The psalmist prays for God's blessing – not for his own benefit, but as a testimony to the world around him.
> Verses 3-5 – The people (Jews) and nations (gentiles) alike are to recognize and praise the Lord.
> Verses 6-7 – Praise to the Lord will release His abundance which will result in the respect of the Lord throughout the whole earth.

Prayer Focus: Lord, help me to always keep Your blessing in the proper perspective as a means to bringing Your blessing to others rather than as a source of prosperity for myself alone. Amen.

Notes:

Spiritual Journal:

Week: Twenty-three
Day: Sunday morning
Book: Psalms
Chapter: Sixty-eight
Memory Verse: One
Principle: This psalm combines some of the elements of the portrait of God victorious yet militant with the image presented in the previous two psalms.  Unlike some earlier psalms which expressed the defeat of the enemy as vengeance, this chapter declares that the military victories lead the enemies to recognize and praise the Lord.  Thus, the psalm becomes the third in a series of testimonies to the nations: the created order, the blessing upon the covenant people, and now the supremacy of the Lord over His enemies.
Outline:
Verses 1-2 – The psalmist calls for the Lord to arise against His enemies.
Verses 3-31 – The Lord deserves praise because His supremacy is evident in every area of activity.
Verses 32-35 – The nations of the earth are called to sing praises to the victorious Lord.
Prayer Focus: Lord, help me to always recognize Your supremacy and to praise You proportionately.  Amen.
Notes:

Spiritual Journal:

Week: Twenty-three
Day: Sunday evening
Book: Psalms
Chapter: Sixty-nine
Memory Verse: Thirty-four
Principle: It is important to acknowledge our fault when our problems are self-imposed.
Outline:

    Verses 1-6 – The psalmist cried out for the Lord's intervention, all the while acknowledging that his problems have been precipitated by his own sins. The negative effect upon others who may be discouraged from following the Lord as a result of the palmist's actions is a serious concern to him.

    Verses 7-12 – The psalmist also declares that his stance for the Lord has precipitated much persecution against him.

    Verses 13-21 – He prays for God to intervene upon his behalf.

    Verses 22-28 – He asks for vengeance against his enemies.

    Verses 29-33 – He promises to give a sacrifice of praise which will be more pleasing than any offering as a thanksgiving for the Lord's deliverance.

    Verses 34-36 – The ultimate victory will be the establishment of the messianic kingdom which is centered in Jerusalem but encompasses the entire creation.

Prayer Focus: Lord, help me to see that every action has reactions throughout the world around me. Help me to live so that the final result of my life will be that I have helped in some way to prepare for Your messianic kingdom. Amen.

Notes:

Spiritual Journal:

Week: Twenty-four
Day: Saturday
Book: Psalms
Chapter: Seventy
Memory Verse: Four
Principle: God delivers because we are poor and needy – not because we are so righteous
or deserving of His help.
Outline:
Verse 1 – The psalmist cries out for help.
Verses 2-3 – He calls for his oppressors to be judged.
Verse 4 – He declares that the response of those who have been redeemed is to
glorify God.
Verse 5 – He reiterates his need for help and stresses that his plea is based on
need, not on his own merit.
Prayer Focus: Lord, help me to be ready to cast myself on Your mercies and not to trust
in my own merits. Amen.
Notes:

Spiritual Journal:

Week: Twenty-four

Day: Sunday morning

Book: Psalms

Chapter: Seventy-one

Memory Verse: Twenty-four

Principle: This psalm is a typical prayer of deliverance with one added element – the sustaining power of God which worked in the psalmist's youth and continues into his old age.

Outline:

Verses 1-5 – The psalmist affirms that the Lord is his refuge and cries out to him for deliverance.

Verse 6 – He introduces the life-long dependence that he has had upon the Lord.

Verses 7-13 – He speaks of the view his enemies have of him and asks God to ensure that they are dismayed as they witness his deliverance.

Verses 14-18 – He commits himself to continually trusting in the Lord because of His constant protection for him and His enduring and continuing provision toward him.

Verses 19-21 – Based on the testimony of the past, the psalmist expects the Lord's intervention in the future.

Verses 22-24 – Exuberant praise will be warranted as the Lord's deliverance is manifested.

Prayer Focus: Lord, help me to remember how You have always delivered, do presently deliver, and have promised to always deliver; furthermore, help me to adequately praise You for Your deliverances.  Amen.

Notes:

Spiritual Journal:

Week: Twenty-four
Day: Sunday evening
Book: Psalms
Chapter: Seventy-two
Memory Verse: Seventeen
Principle: David prays for the favor of God upon himself and upon his son Solomon as they serve as the kings of Israel. The psalm also is prophetic in that it speaks of the messianic reign of Christ as King of kings and Lord of lords.
Outline:
Verse 1 – The psalmist prays for his reign as king and for that of his son.
Verses 2-4 – The blessed character of the son's reign is described.
Verse 5 – There will be an eternal response of the human race to the goodness of God in the messianic reign.
Verses 6-7 – The peace of his reign is picturesquely presented.
Verse 8 – The imagery used to describe the extent of the messianic kingdom portrays it as universal. "From sea to sea" speaks of the Mediterranean (the western boundary of Israel) to the Atlantic (the western frontier of the then-known world). "From the river to the ends of the earth" refers to the Euphrates (the eastern boundary of God's covenant promise to Abraham) to China (the eastern frontier of the then-known world).
Verses 9-11 – The inhabitants of the nations shall show servitude to the messianic king.
Verses 12-14 – His greatness will be established in the graciousness he shows to the needy.
Verses 15-17 – His reign shall be without end.
Verses 18-19 – Praise is obligatory for such a king.
Verse 20 – David affirms that this is his ultimate prayer request.
Prayer Focus: Lord, I desire to see Your kingdom established above all nations; but, most of all, I desire to see it established in my own heart. Amen.
Notes:




Spiritual Journal:

Week: Twenty-five
Day: Saturday
Book: Psalms
Chapter: Seventy-three
Memory Verse: Seventeen
Principle: The inequities of life can only be reconciled when we are instructed in the ways of God.
Outline:
Verses 1-9 – The haughtiness, prosperity, and apparent security of the ungodly are problematic to the psalmist.
Verses 10-14 – It seems that even God is not concerned about the inequities between the righteous and the ungodly.
Verses 15-17 – The psalmist declares that he knows that his concerns are unfounded and that the answer to the questions is found in the instruction of the Lord.
Verses 18-20 – He declares that the end of the matter will be a just and speedy judgment of the wicked.
Verses 21-26 – The psalmist acknowledges that his concerns were improper and reconfirms his faith in and dependence upon the Lord.
Verses 27-28 – The final ends of the righteous and the wicked are contrasted.
Prayer Focus: Lord, help me to always trust in You even when the present evidence doesn't seem to make sense.   Amen.
Notes:

Spiritual Journal:

Week: Twenty-five
Day: Sunday morning
Book: Psalms
Chapter: Seventy-four
Memory Verse: Twenty-two
Principle: The oppression of God's people is an offense against God Himself; He will avenge for His own sake.
Outline:
> Verses 1-11 – The psalmist describes the conditions imposed upon the nation and people of God by the invading enemy, and he asks why God has allowed it to be so.
>
> Verses 12-17 – Through reciting the sovereignty of God and some of His great historic acts of authority, the psalmist questions why God does not act immediately to rectify the situation.
>
> Verses 18-21 – The wickedness of the oppressor and the covenant relationship of the oppressed are cited in the request for God to act.
>
> Verses 22-23 – The ultimate call for action is couched in light of the fact that the offenses are against God Himself.

Prayer Focus: Lord, always help me to remember that when I (as the apple of Your eye) am offended, it is also an offense against You.   Amen.
Notes:

Spiritual Journal:

Week: Twenty-five
Day: Sunday evening
Book: Psalms
Chapter: Seventy-five
Memory Verse: Two
Principle: As a fitting conclusion to the trilogy with the previous two psalms, this chapter declares that God has acted in His proper time to right the inequities of life.
Outline:

Verses 1-3 – The psalmist praises God for acting in the proper time to avenge his situation.

Verses 4-5 – The wicked are reminded that they were warned of the coming judgment.

Verses 6-10 – Judgment of the wicked oppressor is accompanied by the exaltation of the oppressed righteous.

Prayer Focus: Lord, help me to always be willing to trust You that You know the proper time for Your intervention. Amen.
Notes:

Spiritual Journal:

Week: Twenty-six
Day: Saturday
Book: Psalms
Chapter: Seventy-six
Memory Verse: Nine

Principle: In previous psalms, we have seen that the psalmist desired the Lord to avenge the righteous far sooner than He chose to move. God's delay was because of His patient desire to give man as gracious a chance as possible to repent. However, there is a limit to the longsuffering of God. Once His anger has reached its threshold, God acts with vengeance against the oppressor.

Outline:
Verses 1-6 – The psalmist describes the victorious authority of the Lord.

Verses 7-9 – The vengeance of the Lord comes at the point when His anger exceeds His longsuffering.

Verses 10-12 – Using the imagery of the tribute received from subdued kingdoms, the psalmist describes the obedience men must give to the Lord.

Prayer Focus: Lord, help me to always make honest vows to You and to be diligent to keep them. Amen.

Notes:



Spiritual Journal:

Week: Twenty-six

Day: Sunday morning

Book: Psalms

Chapter: Seventy-seven

Memory Verse: Fourteen

Principle: There are times in our lives when it seems that God is not on our side and has not only failed to act on our behalf but has rather chosen to act against us. In times like these, we must call back to memory the testimonies of His previous miraculous intervention. The past deliverances bring present faith and future hope.

Outline:

Verses 1-6 – The psalmist recites his supplication unto the Lord and the Lord's response to his plea.

Verses 7-9 – He questions the Lord's present seeming abandonment.

Verses 10-15 – He encourages himself with the testimonies of the Lord's wondrous works and majestic person.

Verses 16-20 – Even nature testifies of the Lord's majesty in delivering His people. Two examples – the opening of the Red Sea and the thunderous appearance of God on Mount Sinai – testify to His authority.

Prayer Focus: Lord, help me to be able to encourage myself by never forgetting how You have always acted on behalf of Your beloved. Amen.

Notes:

Spiritual Journal:

Week: Twenty-six
Day: Sunday evening
Book: Psalms
Chapter: Seventy-eight
Memory Verse: Seventy-two
Principle: In many of the previous psalms, we have dealt with the external enemies of God; in this psalm, we focus on the internal disobedience of His own people. It is amazing how that we can rebel against God even in the midst of His blessings.
Outline:
Verses 1-4 – The psalmist invokes the testimonies of the previous generations to teach the present and future generations.
Verses 5-8 – He emphasizes that the covenant established with the fathers was for the benefit of all coming generations.
Verses 9-20 – He illustrates the rebelliousness of the people by giving examples of their turning not only from God but also against Him – even in the midst of His blessings upon them.
Verses 21-31 – The loving nature of God is demonstrated in His continuance of blessing upon the people even though His anger was kindled and He acted justly in bringing judgment upon them.
Verses 32-39 – Even with their continued rebellion and their sometimes half-hearted return to Him, the Lord's compassion was extended to His people.
Verses 40-72 – In a rather lengthy discourse, the psalmist recites the history of God's miraculous acts on behalf of His people and their continued rejection of Him. The concluding verse, which refers to the righteous leadership of King David, seems also to be an allusion to the integrity of God Himself in His caring for His people.
Prayer Focus: Lord, help me to never accept Your blessings and fail to love the Blesser. Amen.
Notes:




Spiritual Journal:

Week: Twenty-seven
Day: Saturday
Book: Psalms
Chapter: Seventy-nine
Memory Verse: Nine
Principle: God's own nature is the foundation for the restoration of His people.
Outline:

       Verses 1-4 – The psalmist delineates the destruction and judgment which have come upon the people.

       Verses 5-7 – He questions God as to when He will be willing to reverse the judgment against them.

       Verses 8-10 – He calls upon the reputation of God Himself as grounds for God to act on behalf of His people.

       Verses 11-13 – He pleads for judgment against the enemies and for salvation for the people on the basis that they are God's people chosen to give praise to Him.

Prayer Focus: Lord, help me to constantly and consistently pursue You for who You are and who I am as Your chosen one.  Amen.

Notes:

Spiritual Journal:

Week: Twenty-seven
Day: Sunday morning
Book: Psalms
Chapter: Eighty
Memory Verse: Nineteen
Principle: Even in the midst of God's wrath and judgment, there is always the promise of
    His restoration.
Outline:
    Verses 1-7 – The psalmist calls upon God for restoration based on the fact that He
        is the good shepherd – foreshadowing the words of Jesus in John chapter
        ten.
    Verses 8-18 – He invokes the imagery of a vine having been planted by the Lord
        and needing to be nurtured and preserved by the husbandman –
        foreshadowing the words of Jesus in John chapter fifteen.
    Verse 19 – The ultimate plea is simply for God to act in restoration.
Prayer Focus: Lord, first of all I would pray that I would be able to abide in Your grace
    so that I never need restoration; but most of all, I ask that You help me to always
    respond quickly to You as my restorer.   Amen.
Notes:




Spiritual Journal:

Week: Twenty-seven
Day: Sunday evening
Book: Psalms
Chapter: Eighty-one
Memory Verse: Thirteen
Principle: It is God's desire that we would recognize His authority in our lives. He wants to deliver us, but He wants us to respond with obedience.
Outline:

       Verses 1-5 – We are commanded to praise and worship the Lord whose concern for our lives was demonstrated in our deliverance from Egypt.

       Verses 6-10 – The Lord Himself speaks and reminds us of His deliverance and asks that we obey some very simple commandments such as recognizing that He alone is God.

       Verses 11-16 – Those who received God's greatest blessings refused to acknowledge Him. All the while, He was reaching out to bless them.

Prayer Focus: Lord, help me to always see not only Your hand of blessing but also Your place of authority in my life. Amen.
Notes:

Spiritual Journal:

Week: Twenty-eight
Day: Saturday
Book: Psalms
Chapter: Eighty-two
Memory Verse: One
Principle: God gives His people a role in administering His judgment and justice in the world. However, we do not judge with truth and equity as He does. Therefore, we stand in His judgment for our lack of righteous decisions.
Outline:
Verse 1 – The Lord is declared as the Judge over all human judges.
Verse 2 – He asks how long we will fail in our responsibility to administer judgment.
Verses 3-4 – The responsibility of righteous judgment is delineated.
Verse 5 – The lack of wisdom of human judges is declared.
Verses 6-7 – Even though God established them in positions of authority, the human judges will be demoted because they failed in their responsibilities.
Verse 8 – The psalmist pleads that the only true Judge – God Himself – will arise in judgment and justice.
Prayer Focus: Lord, help me to hear from You any time I am required to speak or act for You. Amen.
Notes:




Spiritual Journal:

Week: Twenty-eight

Day: Sunday morning

Book: Psalms

Chapter: Eighty-three

Memory Verse: Eighteen

Principle: In praying for deliverance from our enemies, we must remember to also pray for their deliverance from their enemy – the devil himself who has deceived them into fighting against God.

Outline:

Verses 1-8 – The psalmist beckons God to act in that the enemies have determined to fight against Him and His people.

Verses 9-12 – The past victories against the enemies are recalled as testimonies of encouragement in the present conflict.

Verses 13-18 – In all the judgment that must be inflicted upon the enemies of God and His people, the ultimate objective is not that they be destroyed but that they would recognize the Lord.

Prayer Focus: Lord, help me to pray for, rather than about, my oppressors.   Amen.

Notes:




Spiritual Journal:

Week: Twenty-eight
Day: Sunday evening
Book: Psalms
Chapter: Eighty-four
Memory Verse: Ten
Principle: Living in the presence of the Lord brings blessing in every area of our lives.
Outline:

        Verses 1-2 – The psalmist declares his love and desire for the presence of God.

        Verses 3-4 – He says that even the birds which nest in the Temple are happy and blessed.

        Verses 5-7 – All who seek after God are blessed.  Even when they pass through the Valley of Baca (weeping), God turns it to a place of blessing and refreshing.

        Verses 8-9 – The psalmist calls upon God to hear his prayer.

        Verse 10 – He determines to live in the presence of the Lord.

        Verses 11-12 – In trusting in the Lord, God's blessings penetrate every area of our lives and we receive every good thing from His hand.

Prayer Focus: Lord, it is often too easy to dwell on other things; help me to never shift my focus from You.  I want to dwell in Your presence and live in Your blessing. Amen.

Notes:



Spiritual Journal:

Week: Twenty-nine
Day: Saturday
Book: Psalms
Chapter: Eighty-five
Memory Verse: Nine
Principle: It is because of God's mercy (His favorable graciousness even when we don't deserve it) that His blessings are extended to His people.
Outline:

Verses 1-3 – Because of God's favor, the sins of His people are forgiven.

Verses 4-7 – The psalmist expresses his obvious dependency upon the mercy of the Lord.

Verses 8-9 – He also expresses the obvious necessity for the people of God to hear and fear the Lord in response to His mercy.

Verses 10-13 – Mercy, truth, and righteousness from the Lord bring increase to the people of God.

Prayer Focus: Lord, I recognize that, without Your unearned grace, I am hopeless; therefore, I trust in Your mercy.   Amen.
Notes:

Spiritual Journal:

Week: Twenty-nine
Day: Sunday morning
Book: Psalms
Chapter: Eighty-six
Memory Verse: Five
Principle: Based solely on the gracious nature of God can we expect His deliverance.
Outline:

> Verses 1-7 – The psalmist recognizes the goodness and abundant mercy of God as the foundation of his request for God's intervention.
>
> Verses 8-10 – The sovereignty of God as the unique majesty of the universe is the foundation of the psalmist's faith.
>
> Verses 11-13 – The psalmist asks for a greater understanding of the Lord so that he can trust Him more.
>
> Verses 14-17 – Based on his revelation of the good nature of God, the psalmist trusts Him for deliverance.

Prayer Focus: Lord, help me to know You better so that I can trust You more.   Amen.
Notes:

Spiritual Journal:

Week: Twenty-nine
Day: Sunday evening
Book: Psalms
Chapter: Eighty-seven
Memory Verse: Three
Principle: As other Old Testament writers confirm, Jerusalem – the place where God has chosen to place His name – is unique in God's favor.
Outline:
Verses 1-3 – The psalmist declares the exalted favor of Jerusalem.
Verses 4-6 – No matter where in the world they may be, those who were born in Jerusalem have a special recognition from God.
Verse 7 – Songs of celebration honor this special city.
Prayer Focus: Lord, as I have learned in another psalm, I pray for the peace of Jerusalem and claim the promise of prosperity which is given to those who love the city. Amen.
Notes:

Spiritual Journal:

Week: Thirty
Day: Saturday
Book: Psalms
Chapter: Eighty-eight
Memory Verse: Ten

Principle: This psalm, which is often associated with the heart cry of Jesus during the night of His trial leading to the crucifixion, asks the question if the dead can praise God. The original intent of this passage was that it would be impossible for praises to come from beyond the grave. However, the prophetic impact of this psalm is that, through Jesus' death, there is victorious praise which overcomes death.

Outline:

Verses 1-5 – The psalmist cries out for God's intervention as he approaches death.

Verses 6-9 – The anguish of the moment is attributed to God – a prophetic allusion to the suffering and death of Christ which were directly part of God's plan of salvation.

Verses 10-12 – The question of praise from beyond the grave is raised.

Verses 13-18 – The seeming abandonment by God and friends expands the agony prophesied by the twenty-second psalm's exclamation, "My God, my God, why have You forsaken Me?"

Prayer Focus: Lord, help me to never fear nor languish over death for I know that in Christ the sting of death has been removed. Amen.

Notes:

Spiritual Journal:

Week: Thirty

Day: Sunday morning

Book: Psalms

Chapter: Eighty-nine

Memory Verse: Thirty-four

Principle: The covenant of God is irrevocable; He will never renege on His Word, regardless of how conditions may change.

Outline:

Verses 1-2 – The psalmist proclaims a perpetual trust and rejoicing because of the unchangeable nature of God's covenant promises.

Verses 3-4 – God Himself speaks of the confirmed stability of His covenant.

Verses 5-14 – The unquestionable sovereignty of the Lord is described.

Verses 15-18 – The position of exalted favor for those who trust God is described.

Verses 19-29 – The covenant with David is delineated.

Verses 30-37 – The covenant supersedes man's ability or desire to fulfill his part of the contract.

Verses 38-45 – God's judgment on covenant breakers is depicted.

Verses 46-51 – The psalmist asks the question as to when God will end His judgment and execute His covenant.

Verse 52 – The psalm concludes with the summation that God is to be eternally praised.

Prayer Focus: Lord, help me to constantly trust in Your unchangeable covenant promises. Amen.

Notes:

Spiritual Journal:

Week: Thirty
Day: Sunday evening
Book: Psalms
Chapter: Ninety
Memory Verse: Seventeen
Principle: Man must always keep his short lifetime in perspective of eternity.
Outline:

       Verses 1-2 – God, who is known elsewhere as the Ancient of Days, predates all creation.

       Verses 3-6 – Even a thousand years – longer than even the lifetime of Methuselah, the longest-living man – is but an instant compared to the eternity of God.

       Verses 7-12 – The shortness of man's life should motivate him to avoid sin which results in the eternal judgment of God.

       Verses 13-17 – The psalmist prays that his life would be characterized by the manifestation of the presence of God.

Prayer Focus: Lord, help me to always remember the eternal consequences of the actions – both good and evil – which I take in my limited lifetime.  Amen.
Notes:

Spiritual Journal:

Week: Thirty-one
Day: Saturday
Book: Psalms
Chapter: Ninety-one
Memory Verse: One
Principle: Trusting in God results in a shield of protection around His people.
Outline:

Verses 1-4 – God provides a place of safety around those who serve Him.

Verses 5-6 – There is no reason to fear when God is our protector.

Verses 7-8 – Even though destruction may come upon those around us who do not serve the Lord, no danger can come upon those under God's protection.

Verses 9-13 – The psalmist gives a variety of conditions in which the Lord's protection is manifest.

Verses 14-16 – God Himself speaks to affirm that He will protect and defend His people.

Prayer Focus: Lord, thank you for that shield of faith which You have set up around me. Amen.

Notes:

Spiritual Journal:

Week: Thirty-one
Day: Sunday morning
Book: Psalms
Chapter: Ninety-two
Memory Verse: One
Principle: In everything, we can see the hand of God perfecting His excellent will; therefore, we should praise Him in all things and at all times.
Outline:
Verses 1-4 – God is worthy to receive our continual praise.
Verses 5-6 – The foolish do not understand the thoughts and ways of God.
Verses 7-11 – The wicked are put down before the Lord.
Verses 12-15 – The righteous shall prosper and increase.
Prayer Focus: Lord, help me to never miss an opportunity to praise You.   Amen.
Notes:




Spiritual Journal:

Week: Thirty-one
Day: Sunday evening
Book: Psalms
Chapter: Ninety-three
Memory Verse: Five
Principle: The Lord is magnificent and worthy of great praise.
Outline:

        Verses 1-2 – The Lord is great and rules eternally.

        Verses 3-4 – The Lord is mightier than any tumult which may arise.

        Verse 5 – The Lord's Word is unquestionable and holy.

Prayer Focus: Lord, I know that it is humanly impossible to express Your magnificence, but please help me to do so as much as I can.   Amen.
Notes:

Spiritual Journal:

Week: Thirty-two

Day: Saturday

Book: Psalms

Chapter: Ninety-four

Memory Verse: Nineteen

Principle: In all the vicissitudes of life, if we will remember the promises of God, we will have victory.

Outline:

Verses 1-7 – The psalmist cries to the Lord to judge the wicked oppressor.

Verses 8-11 – He declares the foolishness of those who do not recognize God's authority.

Verses 12-15 – In contrast, those who are instructed of the Lord are blessed.

Verses 16-19 – Without the help of the Lord, there would be no hope for deliverance.

Verses 20-23 – Victory is manifest in the Lord.

Prayer Focus: Lord, thank You that You are a very present help in the time of trouble. Amen.

Notes:

Spiritual Journal:

Week: Thirty-two
Day: Sunday morning
Book: Psalms
Chapter: Ninety-five
Memory Verse: Six
Principle: It is possible to live in God's blessing and yet provoke Him by refusing to enter into His full will. The people of Israel did exactly this when they enjoyed their deliverance from Egypt but refused to enter into the Promised Land.
Outline:
Verses 1-6 – The psalmist calls for his readers to praise and worship the Lord.
Verses 7-11 – He declares that we are the flock of God and should not resist His shepherding as did the people of Israel when they refused to go into the Promised Land. He admonishes that we should not fall under the wrath of God as did those who provoked the Lord in the desert of Sinai.
Prayer Focus: Lord, help me to never miss or fail to enter into any of Your promises or blessings. Amen.
Notes:




Spiritual Journal:

Week: Thirty-two
Day: Sunday evening
Book: Psalms
Chapter: Ninety-six
Memory Verse: Four
Principle: Because of who He is and what He does, God is worthy to be praised.
Outline:
> Verses 1-6 – Because God is the only true God, He should be exceedingly praised.
>
> Verses 7-10 – His praise should come from all the nations of the earth.
>
> Verses 11-12 – Nature itself should enter into the praises of God.
>
> Verse 13 – He will judge all men.

Prayer Focus: Lord, my request is that I might be a praiser myself and a catalyst of praise among others.   Amen.
Notes:




Spiritual Journal:

Week: Thirty-three
Day: Saturday
Book: Psalms
Chapter: Ninety-seven
Memory Verse: Six
Principle: As with any coin, there are two sides to the presence of the Lord. To those who do not yield to His authority, He appears as the light of judgmental lightning; to those who love and serve Him, He appears as the light of righteousness and gladness.
Outline:
Verse 1 – The Lord's sovereignty should evoke praise from all the earth.
Verses 2-7 – Those who choose other gods are destroyed before His presence.
Verses 8-12 – For those who love Him, the Lord's presence brings preservation and prosperity.
Prayer Focus: Lord, help me to live in the presence of Your joyous light. Amen.
Notes:

Spiritual Journal:

Week: Thirty-three
Day: Sunday morning
Book: Psalms
Chapter: Ninety-eight
Memory Verse: Four
Principle: Because God will judge with equity, He is worthy to be lavished with praise.
Outline:

> Verses 1-3 – Because of His righteous victories and faithfulness, the Lord is worthy of praise.
>
> Verses 4-6 – Every form of jubilant praise should be given to the Lord.
>
> Verses 7-8 – The created order must enter into the praise celebration.
>
> Verse 9 – It is because of His unerring fairness that He deserves such universal praise.

Prayer Focus: Lord, help me to praise You adequately for all Your worthiness.   Amen.
Notes:

Spiritual Journal:

Week: Thirty-three
Day: Sunday evening
Book: Psalms
Chapter: Ninety-nine
Memory Verse: Five
Principle: To punctuate whatever else we may say about our God, we must proclaim that He is holy.
Outline:
> Verses 1-3 – We must praise God because He reigns and because He is holy.
> Verses 4-5 – We must worship God because He judges with equity and because He is holy.
> Verses 6-9 – We must exalt the Lord because of the testimonies established in His servants of old and because He is holy.
Prayer Focus: Lord, never let me forget that You truly are holy.
Notes:

Spiritual Journal:

Week: Thirty-four
Day: Saturday
Book: Psalms
Chapter: One hundred
Memory Verse: Four
Principle: There are progressive steps to coming into the very presence of God.
Outline:

Verses 1-2 – Coming into the very presence of God can be accomplished through joyous singing.

Verse 3 – It is also necessary to recognize our dependence upon Him and be submissive to His leadership.

Verse 4 – Gratefulness brings us into God's premises, and praise brings us into His courtyard.

Verse 5 – His enduring goodness is reason enough for us to express our thankfulness in songs of praise. It is also the reason that He is willing to invite us into His very presence.

Prayer Focus: Lord, the thing I desire most in life is to be able to enter into Your presence and know You intimately. Amen.

Notes:

Spiritual Journal:

Week: Thirty-four

Day: Sunday morning

Book: Psalms

Chapter: One hundred one

Memory Verse: Two

Principle: Before we can judge others, we must judge ourselves.

Outline:

> Verse 1 – The psalmist declares that he will praise the Lord on two accounts: for His mercy (favor for the repentant) and for His justice (judgment for those who refuse to repent).
>
> Verses 2-4 – He adamantly insists upon keeping himself pure before the Lord.
>
> Verses 5-8 – Acting as the judge appointed in Psalm 82, the author determines that he will execute judgment upon all who deserve it.

Prayer Focus: Lord, help me to always remember to deal with the log in my own eye before I tackle the speck in my neighbor's eye.   Amen.

Notes:

Spiritual Journal:

Week: Thirty-four
Day: Sunday evening
Book: Psalms
Chapter: One hundred two
Memory Verse: Twenty-seven
Principle: Nothing is permanent except God Himself.
Outline:

      Verses 1-2 – The psalmist opens with a prayer for God to intervene and bring change into his situation.

      Verses 3-11 – In describing his difficulties, the psalmist attributes them to the judgment of the Lord; this summation is confirmation that change can come through intercession.

      Verse 12 – The one thing that does not change is the One who can cause change in everything else.

      Verses 13-22 – God will arise and change the plight of His people in prominence among the nations.

      Verses 23-26 – God effects change in individuals and mankind as a whole.

      Verses 27-28 – Only God Himself and those He establishes will remain permanently.

Prayer Focus: Lord, help me to remember that my only hope for permanence is to be established in Your unchangeable love.   Amen.
Notes:

Spiritual Journal:

Week: Thirty-five
Day: Saturday
Book: Psalms
Chapter: One hundred three
Memory Verse: One
Principle: God deserves praises not only in earth but in heaven as well.
Outline:

> Verses 1-2 – The psalmist stirs himself up to bless and praise the Lord.
>
> Verses 3-19 – He lists the benefits for which we should praise the Lord:
>> a) Forgiveness
>> b) Health and healing
>> c) Protection
>> d) Physical, emotional, and spiritual provision
>> e) Righteous judgment
>> f) Revelation
>> g) Abundant mercy
>> h) Covenant surety
>> i) Perpetual sovereignty
>
> Verses 20-21 – The angels are admonished to praise the Lord.
>
> Verse 22 – The creation is to join in praising Him.

Prayer Focus: Lord, help me to constantly be aware of Your benefits and to be consistently vocal in praising You. Amen.

Notes:

Spiritual Journal:

Week: Thirty-five
Day: Sunday morning
Book: Psalms
Chapter: One hundred four
Memory Verse: Thirty-three
Principle: God is the creator and sustainer of the whole earth.   He created it perfectly and
       is worthy of praise from His creation.
Outline:
       Verses 1-4 – God in His majesty is worthy of praise.
       Verses 5-30 – The Lord not only created the universe, He sustains its very
          existence.
       Verses 31-32 – The creation trembles before the awesomeness of God.
       Verses 33-34 – The psalmist determines to sing the Lord's praises.
       Verse 35 – Sinners will be judged but the people of the Lord will live with
          perpetual praise.
Prayer Focus: Lord, as a part of Your creation, I praise You with my whole being.
       Amen.
Notes:




Spiritual Journal:

Week: Thirty-five

Day: Sunday evening

Book: Psalms

Chapter: One hundred five

Memory Verse: One

Principle: Having established that God deserves praise from the creation in general, the psalmist now turns to Israel in specific and demonstrates that He deserves their praise in that He has established and maintained covenant with them.

Outline:

Verses 1-6 – The Jewish race is directed to praise the Lord and testify of His works.

Verses 7-45 – The hand of God over His people Israel is explained.

a) Through His covenant with Abraham

b) Through His protection as they wandered among the nations

c) Through His establishing Joseph in Egypt as a provision for their preservation during the famine

d) Through their increase in Egypt

e) Through their deliverance from Egypt

f) Through the prosperity they took with them as they left the bondage of Egypt

g) Through His guidance and provision as they wandered the Sinai Desert

h) Through their establishment as a nation with divine law as their guidance

Prayer Focus: Lord, help me to remember how You have worked in my life so that I will never fail to praise You.   Amen.

Notes:

Spiritual Journal:

Week: Thirty-six
Day: Saturday
Book: Psalms
Chapter: One hundred six
Memory Verse: Forty-five
Principle: God is totally justified in any punishment He metes out to His people because of their blatant rebellion even in spite of His blessing. However, because of His gracious mercy to keep His covenant, we are pardoned and blessed.
Outline:
      Verse 1 – We must give praise and thanks to God for His eternal mercy.
      Verses 2-3 – The psalmist asks who can adequately respond to God's great mercy.
      Verses 4-5 – The psalmist asks to be included in God's continuing mercy.
      Verses 6-7 – He recognizes his part in the collective sin of the people.
      Verses 8-12 – In spite of the people's sin, God acted on their behalf.
      Verses 13-15 – Even though the people rebelled, God gave them what they wanted even though it destroyed them spiritually.
      Verses 16-43 – The history of Israel is a series of rebellions against God. At one point, it was only the bold intercession of Moses which kept the Lord from eradicating the whole nation.
      Verses 44-46 – In spite of their repeated sin, God continued to show mercy to His people.
      Verses 47-48 – The psalm concludes with a request for salvation and a promise of praise and thanksgiving for the deliverance.
Prayer Focus: Lord, help me not to rebel; but when I do, help me to find Your redeeming mercy. Amen.
Notes:

Spiritual Journal:

Week: Thirty-six
Day: Sunday morning
Book: Psalms
Chapter: One hundred seven
Memory Verse: Forty-three
Principle: The wondrous works of God are testimonials to His intervention in the lives of both the righteous and unrighteous; men should see them and honor God.
Outline:
> Verses 1-9 – The deliverance of the people from Egypt should be cause enough for men to give thanks to God.
>
> Verses 10-16 – When rebelliousness leads men into God's judgment but their repentance brings them to God's mercy, they should recognize the Lord and give Him praise.
>
> Verses 17-22 – God's mercy on the foolish men who refuse Him is reason for men to praise the Lord and give Him thanks.
>
> Verses 23-32 – Men should praise God for the way He delivers the seafarers from the storms.
>
> Verses 33-43 – Because He can bring the high low and exalt the lowly, it is wise to acknowledge Him.

Prayer Focus: Lord, all around me are evidences of Your authority; help me to see them and honor You as I should. Amen.
Notes:

Spiritual Journal:

Week: Thirty-six
Day: Sunday evening
Book: Psalms
Chapter: One hundred eight
Memory Verse: Thirteen
Principle: Recognizing our total dependence upon God is the key to victory over our enemies.
Outline:

       Verses 1-4 – The psalmist declares his intention to sing praises to the Lord among the nations – a prophetic glimpse at the victories he expects to win.

       Verses 5-6 – The psalmist's victories are the Lord's victories.

       Verses 7-9 – He lists the areas of conquest where he expects the Lord to give him victory.

       Verses 10-13 – The psalmist reiterates that, without God's help, he is defeated; but with the assistance of the Lord, he is a great conqueror.

Prayer Focus: Lord, upon You and You alone can I depend.   Amen.
Notes:

Spiritual Journal:

Week: Thirty-seven
Day: Saturday
Book: Psalms
Chapter: One hundred nine
Memory Verse: Four
Principle: Prayer is the only proper response to the inequities we suffer.
Outline:

> Verses 1-5 – The psalmist describes the abuses he has suffered and asks God to hear his prayers about the situation.
>
> Verses 6-20 – He asks God to judge the oppressor in every area of his life, including both his parents and children as well.
>
> Verses 21-27 – He describes his misery and asks for God's mercy to be shown to him for the sake of God's own reputation as a protector and blesser of His people.
>
> Verses 28-31 – The wicked will curse and bear his shame and disgrace; however, the psalmist will praise and enjoy the salvation of the Lord.

Prayer Focus: Lord, I trust in You to execute vengeance accompanied with Your gracious deliverance.   Amen.

Notes:

Spiritual Journal:

Week: Thirty-seven

Day: Sunday morning

Book: Psalms

Chapter: One hundred ten

Memory Verse: One

Principle: This prophetic psalm is referred to several times in the New Testament as a reference to the coming of Christ.

Outline:

        Verses 1-2 – The Messiah is the Lord over King David. He will be established in authority above His enemies and will execute divine rule from Jerusalem.

        Verses 3-4 – In addition to His position as divine king, the Messiah is the divine priest – not after the human order of Aaron, but by the unique appointment of the order of Melchizedek.

        Verses 5-7 – The Messiah shall execute divine judgment upon all nations.

Prayer Focus: Lord, I reverence You as king and priest – not only of the whole world, but specifically of my own life. Amen.

Notes:

Spiritual Journal:

Week: Thirty-seven

Day: Sunday evening

Book: Psalms

Chapter: One hundred eleven

Memory Verse: Ten

Principle: Obeying God's commandments brings wisdom to play in every area of our lives.

Outline:

Verses 1-6 – The psalmist declares that He will give praise to God for all the wondrous works of care for His people.

Verses 7-9 – He praises the attributes of God exhibited through His works:

a) Truth

b) Justice

c) Steadfastness

d) Holiness

e) Redemptiveness

f) Awesomeness

Verse 10 – To be wise, fear the Lord and obey His commandments.

Prayer Focus: Lord, I want to be wise; help me to properly respect and obey You. Amen.

Notes:

Spiritual Journal:

Week: Thirty-eight
Day: Saturday
Book: Psalms
Chapter: One hundred twelve
Memory Verse: One
Principle: Perpetual blessing which extends to his descendants is the heritage of the man who consistently follows the Lord.
Outline:
        Verse 1 – Blessing is pronounced upon the man who constantly puts God in first place in his life.
        Verses 2-10 – His blessings include:
            a) Mighty descendants
            b) Prosperity
            c) Generosity toward others
            d) Discretions
            e) Endurance
            f) Fearless faith
            g) Victory over his enemies
Prayer Focus: Lord, help me to be the righteous man who can inherit such wonderful promises from You.   Amen.
Notes:

Spiritual Journal:

Week: Thirty-eight

Day: Sunday morning

Book: Psalms

Chapter: One hundred thirteen

Memory Verse: Three

Principle: God is worthy of praise not only because He is the majestic ruler of the universe but also because He is the loving caretaker of the poor.

Outline:

Verses 1-3 – We are commanded to praise the Lord at all times.

Verses 4-5 – The exaltation of the Lord is described.

Verses 6-9 – His caring love for and elevation of the poor are portrayed.

Prayer Focus: Lord, I do praise You for Your gracious care for the least of us, Your creatures.   Amen.

Notes:

Spiritual Journal:

Week: Thirty-eight
Day: Sunday evening
Book: Psalms
Chapter: One hundred fourteen
Memory Verse: Seven
Principle: The mighty acts of God require awe from not only mankind but also from the created order.
Outline:
   Verses 1-6 – God's deliverance of Israel out of Egypt evoked a response from the physical order.
   Verses 7-8 – His continuing acts and mighty presence demand awe and respect from all creation.
Prayer Focus: Lord, let me join in with the creation in showing forth Your praises. Amen.
Notes:




Spiritual Journal:

Week: Thirty-nine
Day: Saturday
Book: Psalms
Chapter: One hundred fifteen
Memory Verse: Eighteen
Principle: Idols are lifeless, powerless, and useless; but God is worthy of universal praise.
Outline:

Verse 1 – God, not man, is worthy of praise.

Verses 2-3 – The heathen may question the existence of the God of heaven.

Verses 4-8 – Their idols are nothing and can do nothing.

Verses 9-15 – Israel is directed to trust the Lord so that He can bless and exalt them.

Verse 16 – God has given man an area of authority and responsibility over which he has discretion.

Verses 17-18 – The dead cannot praise God, so the psalmist determines to praise Him while he has the opportunity.

Prayer Focus: Lord, help me to never be fooled in giving honor to anything or anyone other than You. Amen.

Notes:

Spiritual Journal:

Week: Thirty-nine
Day: Sunday morning
Book: Psalms
Chapter: One hundred sixteen
Memory Verse: Five
Principle: Recognizing the hand of God's blessing in our lives should evoke a response of thanksgiving and loyalty from His servants.
Outline:

Verses 1-4 – The psalmist expresses his love for the Lord in response to God's deliverance on his behalf.

Verses 5-11 – The psalmist describes how the Lord has acted on his behalf.

Verses 12-14 – He determines to give proper respect to the Lord in response to His graciousness toward him.

Verse 15 – Even in death, the righteous man is blessed of God.

Verses 16-19 – The psalmist renews his commitment and allegiance to the Lord.

Prayer Focus: Lord, help me to never under evaluate Your graciousness to me when I pay my vows of worship to You.   Amen.
Notes:




Spiritual Journal:

Week: Thirty-nine

Day: Sunday evening

Book: Psalms

Chapters: One hundred seventeen and one hundred eighteen

Memory Verse: Fourteen of chapter one hundred eighteen

Principle: The repeated concept of praise which is due to the delivering Lord is brought into the perspective of messianic salvation through a prophetic reference to the rejection and crucifixion of Christ.

Outline:

Verses 117:1-118:1 – God's mercy requires praise and worship.

Verses 2-18 – The testimony of God's intervention on behalf of His people is repeated.

Verses 19-20 – The promise of an entrance into heaven is declared.

Verses 21-24 – Salvation is attributed to the rejected cornerstone, a prophetic reference to Christ.

Verses 25-29 – Another prophetic reference to the coming of the Messiah as Savior gives us an advance glimpse at the Triumphal Entry on the first Palm Sunday.

Prayer Focus: Lord, help me to never reject You but to always welcome Your coming with salvation. Amen.

Notes:

Spiritual Journal:

Week: Forty
Day: Saturday
Book: Psalms
Chapter: One hundred nineteen verses one through eight
Memory Verse: Two
Principle: The one-hundred-nineteenth psalm, the longest book of the Bible, is a lengthy poem consisting of twenty-two stanzas of eight verses each. The first letter of each line in each stanza begins with the same letter of the Hebrew alphabet so that the entire alphabet is used in constructing the psalm. The over-all theme of the psalm is to exalt the qualities of the Word of God. The first stanza's emphasis is that there is a special blessing for those who serve the Lord whole-heartedly. The psalmist declares his intention to follow the Lord unwaveringly so that he will receive these blessings.

Outline:
Verses 1-4 – The conditions for blessedness are listed.
Verses 5-8 – The psalmist declares his desire to be blessed and his intent to fulfill the Lord's requirements.

Prayer Focus: Lord, I join the psalmist in his desire to be wholly dedicated to You and become a recipient of Your blessing. Amen.

Notes:

Spiritual Journal:

Week: Forty
Day: Sunday morning
Book: Psalms
Chapter: One hundred nineteen verses nine through thirty-two
Memory Verse: Eleven
Principle: Having determined in the first stanza that he wants to receive the blessings afforded to the wholly upright, the psalmist expresses his focus on knowing and following the Law of the Lord. The only key to success in life is to follow the commandments of the Lord.
Outline:

       Verses 9-16 – In order to cleanse his ways, the psalmist dedicates himself to the Word of the Lord.

       Verses 17-24 – He prays for the graciousness of God in that he honors the Word of the Lord while his oppressors do not.

       Verses 25-32 – The psalmist recognizes his dependency upon God to instruct him in the Word even though he has made his own determination to pursue after it.

Prayer Focus: Lord, I understand that it is not just Your Word but also Your Spirit activating it inside of me which will cause me to live properly before You. Amen.
Notes:

Spiritual Journal:

Week: Forty

Day: Sunday evening

Book: Psalms

Chapter: One hundred nineteen verses thirty-three through forty-eight

Memory Verse: Thirty-three

Principle: In the New Testament, we read Paul's summation of this principle: it is the Lord who works in us so that we can both will and do His work.

Outline:

> Verses 33-40 – Even with his determination to observe the Law of the Lord, the psalmist maintains that he is still dependent upon the Lord to provide the result in his life. As the New Testament teaches, salvation is not of works but of God's grace.

> Verses 41-48 – He reiterates his perpetual love for and trust in the Word of the Lord.

Prayer Focus: Lord, help me to become so full of Your Word that I automatically respond according to Your precepts in any situation. Amen.

Notes:

Spiritual Journal:

Week: Forty-one

Day: Saturday

Book: Psalms

Chapter: One hundred nineteen verses forty-nine through seventy-two

Memory Verse: Seventy-two

Principle: There is a way out of trouble; it is to truly love and obey the statutes of the Lord.

Outline:

Verses 49-56 – Encouragement and hope come through remembering and following the precepts of the Lord.

Verses 57-64 – In the midst of persecution and oppression, the psalmist maintains his dedication to God and His instruction.

Verses 65-71 – The psalmist declares that his feelings concerning the Law have been proven through personal experience. They are tried and proven testimonials of the power of the Word of God.

Verse 72 – The instruction of the Lord is more valuable than financial wealth.

Prayer Focus: Lord, I don't want to live by theory; let the truths of Your Word be proven in my life. Amen.

Notes:




Spiritual Journal:

Week: Forty-one

Day: Sunday morning

Book: Psalms

Chapter: One hundred nineteen verses seventy-three through ninety-six

Memory Verse: Ninety-two

Principle: Our security is in being established in the unchangeable Word of God which is established in heaven.

Outline:

> Verses 73-80 – Concentration on the Word of God causes the psalmist to feel security.
>
> Verses 81-88 – In spite of the afflictions he encounters, the psalmist still knows that he is established through his trust in the Word of God.
>
> Verses 89-96 – There is eternal surety in the established Word of God.

Prayer Focus: Lord, help me to live in Your Word and Your will so that I can experience Your all-encompassing security.   Amen.

Notes:

Spiritual Journal:

Week: Forty-one
Day: Sunday evening
Book: Psalms
Chapter: One hundred nineteen verses ninety-seven through one hundred twenty
Memory Verse: One hundred five
Principle: We cannot lean upon our own understanding but must trust in the Lord and follow His Word in all our ways if we hope to succeed in life.
Outline:
>    Verses 97-104 – All true wisdom is rooted in the Word of God.
>    Verses 105-112 – Guidance for our daily lives comes from the Word of God.
>    Verses 113-120 – There is safety from the attacks of the enemy in fearing God's judgment.
Prayer Focus: Lord, like King Solomon, I acknowledge that I do not have the wisdom to go in and out among Your people.  Only by trusting in Your Word can I expect to have my paths directed and my steps led properly.  Amen.
Notes:

Spiritual Journal:

Week: Forty-two

Day: Saturday

Book: Psalms

Chapter: One hundred nineteen verses one hundred twenty-one through one hundred forty-four

Memory Verse: One hundred thirty

Principle: The answer to the request of this passage – that the Lord would teach us to know His Word – is found in the New Testament promise of the coming of the divine teacher – the Holy Spirit.

Outline:

> Verses 121-128 – The psalmist loves the Word of God, yet still feels a need to be instructed in it.
>
> Verses 129-136 – The psalmist expresses the value of the Word of God and says that he is extremely disturbed by those who do not treasure it.
>
> Verses 137-144 – Understanding God's precepts gives us a solution to any and every problem.

Prayer Focus: Lord, help me to rely upon the Holy Spirit's instruction in Your Word. Amen.

Notes:

Spiritual Journal:

Week: Forty-two

Day: Sunday morning

Book: Psalms

Chapter: One hundred nineteen verses one hundred forty-five through one hundred sixty-eight

Memory Verse: One hundred sixty-five

Principle: Intense desire for the Word of God, not a casual acknowledgment of it, is the key to spiritual victory.

Outline:

> Verses 145-152 – The intensity with which the psalmist pursues God and His Word is described.
>
> Verses 153-160 – Respect for and obedience to the Word of God is the difference between the righteous and the ungodly.
>
> Verses 161-168 – Diligence and persistence characterize the psalmist's pursuit of the Word of God.

Prayer Focus: Lord, help me to always pursue You with a fervent faith.   Amen.

Notes:




Spiritual Journal:

Week: Forty-two

Day: Sunday evening

Book: Psalms

Chapter: One hundred nineteen verses one hundred sixty-nine through one hundred seventy-six

Memory Verse: One hundred seventy-two

Principle: As we learn in Joshua, we must never let the Word of God depart from our lips if we wish to have success and prosperity.

Outline:

Verses 169-176 – The psalm concludes with a summation of the psalmist's dependence upon the Word of God and the God of the Word.

Prayer Focus: Lord, help me to not just talk about Your Word but to truly live it.   Amen.

Notes:

Spiritual Journal:

Week: Forty-three
Day: Saturday
Book: Psalms
Chapter: One hundred twenty through one hundred twenty-one
Memory Verse: Two of chapter one hundred twenty-one
Principle: The only place to turn in times of trouble is to God.
Outline:

        Verses 120:1-2 – The psalmist testifies that the Lord has answered when he called upon Him during times of distress.

        Verses 120:3-4 – He muses upon the kind of judgment the wicked deserve.

        Verses 120:5-7 – He describes his condition as a man who would prefer to live peaceably but has been forced by his evil oppressors to resort to warfare.

        Verses 121:1-2 – Having been forced into battle in the last section, the psalmist now asks where he will find help during the conflict. His answer is only in the Lord.

        Verses 121:3-6 – He describes how the Lord will be his constant preserver and defender against both the natural elements and his hostile enemies.

        Verses 121:7-8 – Preservation by the Lord is promised.

Prayer Focus: Lord, help me to look only to You as my source of help. Amen.
Notes:

Spiritual Journal:

Week: Forty-three
Day: Sunday morning
Book: Psalms
Chapter: One hundred twenty-two
Memory Verse: Six
Principle: Jerusalem is a special city with God's individual blessing appointed upon it.
Outline:

> Verses 1-2 – The psalmist expressed his personal joy in relationship to the city of Jerusalem.
>
> Verses 3-5 – The city is uniquely blessed of God.
>
> Verses 6-9 – Blessing, good, peace, and prosperity are appointed to those who love and pray for the city of God.

Prayer Focus: Lord, help me to remember to pray for the city of Jerusalem, especially as it experiences so much violence, terrorism, and strife.   Amen.
Notes:




Spiritual Journal:

Week: Forty-three

Day: Sunday evening

Book: Psalms

Chapter: One hundred twenty-three

Memory Verse: One

Principle: We must diligently and determinately seek the face of God in order to obtain His mercy.

Outline:

 Verses 1-2 – The psalmist describes his intentional concentration and determinate focus on the Lord.

 Verses 3-4 – In his distress, his only hope of salvation is the mercy of God.

Prayer Focus: Lord, in the New Testament, I have learned that I should come boldly into Your presence to obtain Your mercy. I know that I cannot have that bold entrance until I have become personally intimate with You; therefore, I renew my determination to quest for Your face. Amen.

Notes:

Spiritual Journal:

Week: Forty-four
Day: Saturday
Book: Psalms
Chapter: One hundred twenty-four
Memory Verse: Eight
Principle: Considering the historical setting of this psalm can add meaning to it. David, possibly the greatest military leader in Israel's history, proclaims that he would have been a total failure if it had not been for the help of the Lord. What an admonition for us that we should not depend upon our own abilities and resources.

Outline:

Verses 1-2 – The psalmist recognizes that history has been determined by the intervention of the Lord.

Verses 3-5 – He engages in a bit of the "What If" game – what would have happened if God had not been part of the equation? The answer is that Israel would have experienced disastrous defeat.

Verses 6-7 – He praises God for the way He acted to rescue them.

Verse 8 – He reaffirms his dependence upon the Lord.

Prayer Focus: Lord, help me to never be fooled into thinking that I have, can, or will be able to defend myself. Amen.

Notes:

Spiritual Journal:

Week: Forty-four

Day: Sunday morning

Book: Psalms

Chapter: One hundred twenty-five

Memory Verse: Two

Principle: God's actions toward us are totally determined by our actions toward Him. If we trust Him, He will establish us with unshakable permanence; if we resist Him, we will be removed.

Outline:

    Verses 1-2 – The solidity of the mountain range symbolizes both the people of God and the provision of God for His people.

    Verse 3 – The wicked shall not rule over God's people.

    Verses 4-5 – Good is promised to those who are upright in their hearts; those who are not will be eradicated.

Prayer Focus: Lord, I want to be unshakably established in Your grace and mercy. Amen.

Notes:

Spiritual Journal:

Week: Forty-four
Day: Sunday evening
Book: Psalms
Chapter: One hundred twenty-six
Memory Verse: Six
Principle: We must always look at the end which God has intended for us rather than the present condition we may be experiencing.  Jeremiah reminds us that God knows the plans He has for us and that those plans are for a good ending.  Paul reaffirms that, with the final end in sight, the present problems become simply light afflictions.
Outline:
        Verse 1 – When God intervenes, it is so surprising that we can hardly believe that it has really happened.
        Verses 2-3 – The psalmist describes the joy and praise invoked by God's intervention.
        Verse 4 – He prays for God to continue to act on his behalf.
        Verses 5-6 – The psalmist admonishes his readers to look beyond the present sorrow and expect a joyous ending.
Prayer Focus: Lord, help me to look beyond my problems to the promise You are holding out to me.  Amen.
Notes:

Spiritual Journal:

Week: Forty-five

Day: Saturday

Book: Psalms

Chapter: One hundred twenty-seven

Memory Verse: One

Principle: We must recognize that it is not our own efforts which bring results, but God working through and for us that accomplishes anything in our lives. We must also recognize that one way He accomplishes His goal in our lives is through our children.

Outline:

> Verses 1-2 – Unless they are blessed of the Lord, all our efforts are vain and useless.
>
> Verses 3-5 – Our children are our blessings from God and our promise of continued victories.

Prayer Focus: Lord, help me to pull back from trying to accomplish things on my own. Also help me to raise children who will go after me as succeeders, not just successors. Amen.

Notes:

Spiritual Journal:

Week: Forty-five
Day: Sunday morning
Book: Psalms
Chapter: One hundred twenty-eight
Memory Verse: One
Principle: God's blessings have as much or more to do with the blessings in the home as with prosperity in the work place. Unlike many men today who sacrifice their families in order to succeed in their careers, the man who is blessed of God will prosper in both home and business.
Outline:
       Verse 1 – God's blessings extend to every area of our lives.
       Verse 2 – We can be blessed in our business and in all our social relationships.
       Verses 3-4 – Our homes and all family members will be blessed.
       Verse 5 – The blessed man will see his entire nation prosper.
       Verse 6 – Not just longevity, but a peaceful long life is promised.
Prayer Focus: Lord, help me to keep all areas of my life in balance as I focus on obtaining Your promised blessings. Amen.
Notes:




Spiritual Journal:

Week: Forty-five
Day: Sunday evening
Book: Psalms
Chapter: One hundred twenty-nine
Memory Verse: Two
Principle: The oppressor of the righteous cannot prosper continually.
Outline:
>    Verses 1-2 – Even though the oppressor has come many times, he has not been allowed to be permanently established.
>    Verses 3-4 – Because of His righteousness, the Lord has not allowed the oppressor to continue.
>    Verses 5-8 – The psalmist proclaims judgments upon the oppressors:
>    >    a) They are confused.
>    >    b) They are displaced.
>    >    c) They are impermanent (like grass growing on a rooftop without soil in which to establish roots).
>    >    d) No one can pronounce blessing upon them.

Prayer Focus: Lord, help me not to focus on my oppression, but on the deliverance You are providing and the judgment You have determined against my oppressor. Amen.

Notes:

Spiritual Journal:

Week: Forty-six
Day: Saturday
Book: Psalms
Chapter: One hundred thirty
Memory Verse: Three
Principle: Having dealt so much in the psalms concerning deliverance from our external enemies, the psalmist now turns his attention to deliverance from our internal enemy – our own sins.
Outline:
Verses 1-3 – The psalmist acknowledges that he is in desperate need of the Lord's deliverance from his own sinfulness and that it is only the Lord's gracious mercy which even gives him a chance to be saved from his multitude of wrongs.
Verses 4-6 – He testifies that he longingly waits for the Lord's intervention and forgiveness.
Verses 7-8 – He calls for a national repentance and dependency upon God and promises that the Lord will redeem the penitent nation.
Prayer Focus: Lord, help me to not be deceived by focusing on my outward enemies and let my internal enemy subdue me.   Amen.
Notes:


Spiritual Journal:

Week: Forty-six

Day: Sunday morning

Book: Psalms

Chapter: One hundred thirty-one

Memory Verse: Three

Principle: Tranquility of spirit and quietness of soul come from trusting confidently in the Lord.

Outline:

Verses 1-2 – The psalmist testifies that he has trained his soul to quietly trust in God.

Verse 3 – He desires that the nation as a whole would join him in confidently hoping upon the Lord.

Prayer Focus: Lord, help me to use the mighty spiritual weapons which Paul described in II Corinthians chapter ten so that I can take control of my emotions and imaginations in order to truly trust in You. Amen.

Notes:

Spiritual Journal:

Week: Forty-six
Day: Sunday evening
Book: Psalms
Chapter: One hundred thirty-two
Memory Verse: Twelve
Principle: We can boldly trust in whatever covenant promises we have with the Lord; He will never fail to fulfill His end of the bargain and we must dedicate ourselves to fulfilling our part.
Outline:
Verses 1-7 – David reminds God of his determinate attempts to uphold his vows and pledges to the Lord.
Verses 8-10 – He asks for God to act in order that the promises of the covenant can be manifest.
Verses 11-12 – Because of the ongoing provisions of the covenant, David calls the blessings upon his descendants.
Verses 13-14 – The covenant includes the physical location of Israel as well as the people of Israel. The psalmist determines to abide in the physical locale as well as in the spiritual blessing.
Verses 15-18 – The Lord responds to David's entreaty by answering with a confirmation that He will uphold the various provisions of the covenant.
Prayer Focus: Lord, help me to be bold in claiming my covenant privileges. Amen.
Notes:

Spiritual Journal:

Week: Forty-seven
Day: Saturday
Book: Psalms
Chapter: One hundred thirty-three
Memory Verse: One
Principle: Unity and harmony within the body of believers are both pleasant and necessary.
Outline:

       Verse 1 – The psalmist proclaims the value of unity within the church (home or any other unit of believers).

       Verse 2 – He likens the pleasantness of that unity to the oil with which the high priest was anointed. The symbolism is that just as the priest could not minister until he was symbolically anointed with the oil to demonstrate his spiritual anointing, so it must be that the Body of Christ cannot effectively represent the Lord until we come together in the bond of truth and love as the answer to Jesus' prayer that we become one as He and the Father are one.

       Verse 3 – This unity is likened to the dew on Mt. Hermon which is the source of life in Israel because it is the origin of the Jordan River by which all of the land is watered. In like manner, our ability to live and work together is the foundation to the operation of the church.

Prayer Focus: Lord, help me to never fail in recognizing my brothers and sisters in the church. Help me to never fail in cooperating fully and working closely with them. Amen.
Notes:

Spiritual Journal:

Week: Forty-seven
Day: Sunday morning
Book: Psalms
Chapter: One hundred thirty-four
Memory Verse: Two
Principle: The proper response to the majesty of God is perpetual praise.
Outline:

       Verse 1 – The psalmist admonished that the night guards in the Temple fill in the gap during the evening hours when the Temple was not open for priests or people to come and offer prayers or praise.

       Verse 2 – Although the Bible gives no specific formula for worship, lifting up hands is a proper position for worship.

       Verse 3 – Praise accompanied with singing is a pleasant approach to God.

Prayer Focus: Lord, help me to adequately praise You.   Amen.
Notes:

Spiritual Journal:

Week: Forty-seven

Day: Sunday evening

Book: Psalms

Chapter: One hundred thirty-five

Memory Verse: Five

Principle: This psalm, which builds upon the previous one by giving examples of the Lord's mighty acts on behalf of His people, compares the Almighty God of Israel with the impotent gods of the other nations and calls upon God's people individually and corporately to praise Him.

Outline:

Verses 1-3 – Psalm 134 is repeated.

Verses 4-14 – Some of the Lord's mighty acts on behalf of His people are listed.

Verses 15-18 – The impotency of the idol gods of the nations is presented in contrast to the mighty acts of the Lord.

Verses 19-21 – The individual tribes are mentioned in the psalmist's admonition to praise the Lord.

Prayer Focus: Lord, help me to never assume that worship is only a corporate event of the church; help me to always remember that it is my individual duty and privilege as well. Amen.

Notes:

Spiritual Journal:

Week: Forty-eight
Day: Saturday
Book: Psalms
Chapter: One hundred thirty-six
Memory Verse: One
Principle: The mercy (undeserved graciousness) of the Lord endures forever.
Outline:

        Verses 1-3 – The psalmist introduces the chapter with a general summation that the Lord is to be praised because He is eternally and unchangeably merciful.

        Verses 4-25 – In what was originally a responsive reading, the psalmist lists many of God's mighty acts on behalf of His people.

        Verse 26 – A summary verse reiterated the obligation to praise the eternally merciful Lord.

Prayer Focus: Lord, Your mercy has proven to be perpetual in my life; for it, I give You praise. Amen.
Notes:

Spiritual Journal:

Week: Forty-eight
Day: Sunday morning
Book: Psalms
Chapter: One hundred thirty-seven
Memory Verse: Five
Principle: There can be no joy or prosperity when separated from the presence of the
    Lord.
Outline:
       Verses 1-4 – The psalmist describes the sorrow that was in the hearts of the
           Jewish people who had been taken away as slaves to Babylon. Their
           sadness is not in their slavery but in their absence from the land which
           God had given to them.
       Verses 5-6 – The psalmist makes a commitment to never forget the blessedness of
           Jerusalem. He invokes serious judgments upon himself if he does.
       Verses 7-9 – He calls for serious judgments upon those nations which have exiled
           the people Israel from their covenant land.
Prayer Focus: Lord, help me to be as adamant about being continually in Your presence
    as the psalmist was about being in Your covenant land. Let me be just as strong
    against anything which would separate me from You as was the psalmist about
    his own forgetfulness and the people who separated him from his homeland.
    Amen.
Notes:

Spiritual Journal:

Week: Forty-eight
Day: Sunday evening
Book: Psalms
Chapter: One hundred thirty-eight
Memory Verse: Eight
Principle: In everything and at all times, the Lord is on the side of His people.
Outline:
>    Verses 1-2 – The psalmist proclaims his intent to praise and worship the Lord.
>    Verse 3 – He testifies that the Lord has delivered him when He called upon Him.
>    Verses 4-5 – All the kings of the earth would join in praises to God if they were aware of His mighty acts.
>    Verses 6-8 – The Almighty God condescends to the lowliest of His creations and cares for the lowliest of his needs.

Prayer Focus: Lord, help me to always remember that You are always listening for my cry and that You are always ready to act on my behalf.   Amen.
Notes:

Spiritual Journal:

Week: Forty-nine
Day: Saturday
Book: Psalms
Chapter: One hundred thirty-nine
Memory Verse: Twenty-three
Principle: Having focused the preceding chapter on the concept that the Lord knows every detail of the problems which His people face, the psalmist now turns to another facet of that same truth: The Lord knows every detail of the sinful thoughts and actions of His people.
Outline:
Verses 1-6 – The psalmist expresses his astonishment at the concept of the omniscience of God.
Verses 7-13 – He is also awed by the omnipresence of the Lord.
Verses 14-18 – He expresses amazement at the minute and meticulous detail of the Lord's concern for him.
Verses 19-22 – The holiness of God is expressed in His vengeance against the ungodly.
Verses 23-24 – The psalmist invites the Lord to search him and examine his motivations. His prayer is twofold: to be purified of anything which would offend the Lord and that he would be established permanently in the grace of the Lord.
Prayer Focus: Lord, I join the psalmist in his prayer that You would search my inward parts and reveal anything in me which does not please You. Amen.
Notes:




Spiritual Journal:

Week: Forty-nine
Day: Sunday morning
Book: Psalms
Chapter: One hundred forty
Memory Verse: Seven
Principle: It is never too often to remind ourselves that the Lord is on the side of the righteous and that He will deliver them and judge the wicked.
Outline:
>    Verses 1-5 – The psalmist calls upon the Lord to deliver him from the evil men who have plotted against him.
>    Verses 6-7 – He continues to express his dependence upon the Lord.
>    Verses 8-11 – He asks for judgment to be meted out against the wicked.
>    Verses 12-13 – He rests in the assurance that the Lord will uphold and establish the righteous.

Prayer Focus: Lord, help me to live righteously so that I can trust in Your deliverance. Amen.
Notes:

Spiritual Journal:

Week: Forty-nine
Day: Sunday evening
Book: Psalms
Chapter: One hundred forty-one
Memory Verse: Three
Principle: In prayer for deliverance from the evil oppressor, it is important to also search our own hearts for evil within ourselves. Jesus taught us this same principle in the Lord's Prayer when He added that we not walk into temptation to the request that we be delivered from evil.
Outline:
        Verses 1-2 – The psalmist asks that his prayer be heard.
        Verses 3-4 – Apparently as a condition for the hearing of his requests, he also petitions that the Lord help him guard his words, intents, and actions.
        Verse 5 – He willingly submits himself to correction of the righteous because his prayer is only for the judgment of the unrighteous.
        Verses 6-10 – He prays that the wicked will not escape the justice due them for their cruel deeds against him.
Prayer Focus: Lord, help me to find righteous men to whom I can be accountable as I seek to live equitably in this inequitable world. Amen.
Notes:

Spiritual Journal:

Week: Fifty
Day: Saturday
Book: Psalms
Chapter: One hundred forty-two
Memory Verse: Five
Principle: No matter where we may look, our only hope is to be found in the Lord.
Outline:

Verses 1-5 – The psalmist reaffirms that, in all his distress, he found no help except in the Lord.

Verses 6-7 – He petitions the Lord for deliverance.

Prayer Focus: Lord, I do acknowledge that there is no one except You who is able or willing to help me.   Amen.
Notes:



Spiritual Journal:

Week: Fifty

Day: Sunday morning

Book: Psalms

Chapter: One hundred forty-three

Memory Verse: Ten

Principle: The servant of the Lord who is seriously seeking to have his heart and ways purged by God can expect the Lord to act on his behalf.

Outline:

 Verses 1-2 – The psalmist acknowledges that he doesn't deserve God's mercy, but he pleads for the Lord's gracious faithfulness.

 Verses 3-6 – Especially in the time of trouble, he seeks diligently after the Lord.

 Verses 7-12 – His prayer for deliverance is seasoned with his desire to know how to perfectly follow the ways of the Lord.

Prayer Focus: Lord, I need to better serve You so that I can better live in Your blessing and provision.   Amen.

Notes:

Spiritual Journal:

Week: Fifty
Day: Sunday evening
Book: Psalms
Chapter: One hundred forty-four
Memory Verse: Fifteen
Principle: It is almost unimaginable that Infinite God Himself is interested in the well-being of finite humans; yet those who call upon Him are abundantly blessed.
Outline:
        Verses 1-2 – The psalmist praises God for giving him the ability to subdue his enemies.
        Verses 3-4 – He expresses his amazement that God is interested in and involved with finite man.
        Verses 5-6 – The magnitude of the Lord's majesty is portrayed.
        Verses 7-8 – The Lord uses His greatness on behalf of His servant.
        Verses 9-10 – The psalmist dedicates a new song of praise to the Lord.
        Verses 11-15 – He spells out the blessings in his family, finances, and emotions which the Lord establishes when the oppressors are removed.
Prayer Focus: Lord, I do stand amazed that the very God of the whole universe can be interested in acting on behalf of such a seemingly insignificant man such as I am. Thank you.  Amen.
Notes:

Spiritual Journal:

Week: Fifty-one
Day: Saturday
Book: Psalms
Chapter: One hundred forty-five
Memory Verse: Eight
Principle: God is worthy of praise because of His personal character as well as His gracious acts.
Outline:

> Verses 1-2 – The psalmist expresses his determination to continually praise the Lord and to enumerate His qualities.
>
> Verses 3-7 – The praises of God should be proclaimed by all men everywhere and at all times.
>
> Verses 8-9 – The graciously loving mercy of the Lord is the motivating force behind all His actions.
>
> Verses 10-13 – The Kingdom of God will be characterized by praise emanating from all men.
>
> Verses 14-21 – The psalmist will praise the Lord because of His loving watchcare for His people.

Prayer Focus: Lord, help me to never forego an opportunity to praise You.   Amen.
Notes:

Spiritual Journal:

Week: Fifty-one
Day: Sunday morning
Book: Psalms
Chapter: One hundred forty-six
Memory Verse: Five
Principle: We will be disappointed if we rely upon men, but our dependence upon God will never fail.
Outline:
Verses 1-2 – The psalmist reiterates his determination to praise the Lord.
Verses 3-4 – He demonstrates the fallacy of trusting in impermanent men.
Verses 5-10 – Security and happiness come from trusting in the omnipotent, omniscient, omnipresent, and all-loving God.
Prayer Focus: Lord, sometimes it is just too easy to trust in visible and tangible sources; help me to have the faith and vision to trust in the invisible, yet almighty, God. Amen.
Notes:

Spiritual Journal:

Week: Fifty-one

Day: Sunday evening

Book: Psalms

Chapter: One hundred forty-seven

Memory Verse: Eleven

Principle: Even though we sometimes cannot see it or sometimes wonder how it can be, God is in direct control of every aspect of creation.

Outline:

Verses 1-6 – We are admonished to praise the Lord because:

a) He has chosen and established Israel.

b) He heals our emotional and physical injuries.

c) He rules the entire universe.

d) He cares for the weak and judges the wicked.

Verses 7-11 – We are admonished to sing to the Lord because:

a) He is in control of nature.

b) He is beyond being impressed by men's strength.

c) He cares for those who rely upon Him.

Verses 12-20 – We are admonished to praise the Lord because:

a) He gives peace and prosperity to His people.

b) He is in control of the natural elements and weather.

c) He has given special revelation of Himself and His will to Israel.

Prayer Focus: Lord, help me to understand all the reasons I have for praising You. Amen.

Notes:

Spiritual Journal:

Week: Fifty-two
Day: Saturday
Book: Psalms
Chapter: One hundred forty-eight
Memory Verse: Thirteen
Principle: The Lord should receive praise from every element of creation.
Outline:

       Verses 1-2 – The angels should praise the Lord.

       Verses 3-6 – The heavenly universe is to praise the Lord.

       Verses 7-10 – The earthly creation is to praise Him.

       Verses 11-12 – Humans of every position must praise Him.

       Verses 13-14 – Special praise should come from His chosen people Israel.

Prayer Focus: Lord, I remember that Jesus taught that the stones would cry out praises if Your people fail to praise You; help me to never forfeit my privilege of praise to a rock.   Amen.

Notes:

Spiritual Journal:

Week: Fifty-two
Day: Sunday morning
Book: Psalms
Chapter: One hundred forty-nine
Memory Verse: One
Principle: Praise can take on two surprisingly different dimensions: jubilant celebration and execution of judgment upon those who oppose the Lord.
Outline:

       Verses 1-5 – Festive praise to the Lord is encouraged.

       Verses 6-9 – Execution of vengeance upon the enemies of God is described as a form of praise to the Lord.

Prayer Focus: Lord, I want to show forth Your praises not only in how I sing and dance before You but also in the way I attack Your enemies – beginning with sinfulness in my own life.   Amen.
Notes:

Spiritual Journal:

Week: Fifty-two
Day: Sunday evening
Book: Psalms
Chapter: One hundred fifty
Memory Verse: Six
Principle: Every form of musical instrument and expression of emotion should be used to praise the Lord.
Outline:
Verse 1 – In the church and in the universe as a whole, the Lord is to be praised.
Verse 2 – He deserves praises because of who He is and because of what He does.
Verses 3-5 – Every means of expression available to us should be used to praise the Lord.
Verse 6 – Every breathing thing should praise the Lord.
Prayer Focus: Lord, help me to be creative and resourceful in my praise to You, not overlooking any means of praise available to me. Amen.
Notes:

Spiritual Journal:

# Teach All Nations Mission

Teach All Nations Mission (TAN) is a global evangelical educational ministry birthed from the teaching ministries of Delron and Peggy Shirley. The name for Teach All Nations Mission was chosen to carefully indicate the exact heart of the Shirleys' mission. TAN's commitment is to establish a solid biblical foundation in national pastors and leaders so they can help enrich their own people. This vision is being accomplished by holding national leadership conferences and publishing and distributing Christian teaching materials in English and their local languages.

Someone accurately observed concerning the revival that is occurring in many parts of our world today that it is a mile wide but only an inch deep – the result of energetic evangelism by both missionaries and local Christians. Sadly, there is a marked shortage of teachers who are taking the next step in fulfilling our Lord's directive to teach them how to observe all that He has commanded. Therefore, Teach All Nations Mission has literally taken the words of Christ from Matthew 28:19, "Teach all nations," as its motto and mission statement.

TAN's commitment is to deepen that revival by training the pastors and leaders who then go back and strengthen their congregations. TAN pays for the travel and lodging of handpicked leaders because Delron and Peggy want to invest into their lives but know that these third-world saints could never afford to come at their own expense. TAN always provides the meals for all the guests during these conferences. The ministry also furnishes solid Christian literature in their local language or in English for those who understand the language.

Delron and Peggy realize that the challenge is much bigger than what they can accomplish in person; therefore, they have determined to expand the scope of their vision. One area of expansion includes a scholarship fund that will allow selected individuals to obtain a formal education in solid Christian colleges and Bible schools or through correspondence courses. The ministry has also assisted in building a Christian school in Zimbabwe and a Bible college in Nepal. Additionally, Teach All Nations assists the pastors and leaders they work with in times of need such as the tsunami in Sri Lanka, the earthquake in Nepal, and hurricanes in Belize and in the Turks and Caicos Islands. More recently, the ministry supported suffering Christians in twelve different nations who lost their source of income during the shutdowns during the COVID-19 pandemic.

Your gifts to and prayers for Teach All Nations will help the Shirleys continue their outreach to Christian leadership around the world.

Teach All Nations Mission
3210 Cathedral Spires
Colorado Springs, CO 80904
719-685-9999
www.teachallnationsmission.com
teachallnations@msn.com

# Books by Delron & Peggy Shirley

Bingo, a Fresh Look at Grace
Christmas Thoughts
Cornerstones of Faith
Daily Bible Study Series (Five-Volume Set)
Daily Ditties from Delron's Desk
(Eight Volumes Available)
Doctor Livingstone, I Presume
Don't Leave Home Without It
Finally, My Brethren
Getting More UMPH out of Your Bible
Going Deeper in Jesus
The Great Commission – Doable
The IN Factors
In This Sign Conquer
Interface
Israel, Key to Human Destiny
The Last Enemy
Lessons Along the Way
Lessons from the Life of David
Living for the End Times
Maturing into the Full Stature of Jesus Christ
Maximum Impact
No Longer Bound
The Non-Conformer's Trilogy
Of Kings and Prophets
Passion for the Harvest
People Who Make A Difference
Positioned for Blessing and Power
Problem People of the Bible
Seeds and Harvest
The Seventh Man at the Well
So Send I You
So, You Wanna be a Preacher
Thirty-, Sixty-, One-Hundred-Fold
Tread Marks
Turning the World Upside Down and Back Again
Verse for the Day (Four Volumes Available)
Women for the Harvest
You'll be Darned to Heck
if You Don't Believe in Gosh
You Can Be Healed
Your Home Can Survive in the 21st Century
Your Part in the Grand Scheme of Things

**Available at:**
**teachallnationsmission.com**